Black Classics

The Wonderful Adventures of Mrs Seacole in Many Lands

Mary Seacole

Published by *Black Classics*
An imprint of The X Press
PO Box 25694, London N17 6TR
Tel: 020 8801 2100
Fax: 020 8885 1322
Email: vibes@xpress.co.uk
Web site: www. xpress.co.uk

Printed by in United Kingdom by Bookmarque

Distributed in UK by Turnaround Distribution, Unit 3, Olympia Trading Estate,
Coburg Road, London N22 6TZ
Tel: 0181 829 3000
Fax: 0181 881 5088

ISBN 1-874509-85-9

Preface to 1857 edition

I should have thought that no preface would have been required to introduce Mrs. Seacole to the British public, or to recommend a book which must, from the circumstances in which the subject of it was placed, be unique in literature.

If singleness of heart, tru charity, and Christian works; if trials and sufferings, dangers and perils, encountered boldly by a helpless woman on her errand of mercy in the camp and in the battlefield, can excite sympathy or move curiosity, *The Wonderful Adeventures of Mrs Seacole in Many Lands* will have many friends and many readers.

Mary Seacole is a plain truth-speaking woman who has lived an adventurous life amid scenes which have never yet found a historian among the actors on the stage where they passed.

I trust that England will not forget one who nursed her sick and sought out her wounded to aid and succour them.

W.H. Russell

About Mary Seacole

Born in Jamaica during slavery, Mary Jane Grant Seacole died in prosperous circumstances on May 14, 1881 and was buried in St. Mary's Catholic Cemetery in London. During her lifetime, she became the most revered and respected black woman in the British Empire for her work with the sick and wounded of the Crimean wars. Unlike Florence Nightingale who built a hospital in relative safety from the scene of battle, Mary Seacole stayed on the front line at the siege of Sebastopol risking her own life to care for the British Army's casualties, and sharing with them the horrors of one of history's most brutal conflicts.

On her return to England, she was the toast of nineteenth century London society and cultivated a friendship with the Princess of Wales, for whom she worked as a masseuse.

What makes this fast-paced and rivetting account of her private and public 'adventures' so unputdownable, is her willingness to confess to feelings that many women of her time, white or black, would have concealed.

Marcia Williams, *Author*

CHAPTER 1

I was born in the town of Kingston, in the island of Jamaica, some time in the present century. As a female, and a widow, I may be well excused giving the precise date of this important event. But I do not mind confessing that the century and myself were both young together, and that we have grown side by side into age and consequence.

I am a Creole, and have good Scotch blood coursing in my veins. My father was a soldier from an old Scotch family. To him I often trace my affection for camp life and my sympathy with what I have heard my friends call the pomp, pride, and circumstance of glorious war. Many people have also traced to my Scotch blood that energy and activity which are not always found in the Creole race, and which have carried me to so many varied scenes. Perhaps they are right. I have often heard the term 'lazy Creole' applied to my country people, but I am sure I do not know what it is to be indolent. All my life long I have followed the impulse which led me to be up and doing and so far from resting idle anywhere. I have never lacked inclination to rove, nor will powerful enough to find a way to carry out my wishes. That these qualities have led me into many countries and brought me into some strange and amusing adventures, the reader, if he or she has the patience to get through this book, will see. Some people, indeed, have called me quite a female Ulysses. I believe that they intended it as a compliment; but from my experience of the Greeks, I do not consider it a very flattering one.

It is not my intention to dwell at any length upon the recollections of my childhood. My mother kept a boarding-house and was, like very many of the Creole women, an admirable doctress, in high repute with the officers of both services, who were from time to time stationed at Kingston. It was very natural that I should inherit her tastes, and so I had from early youth a yearning for medical knowledge and practice which has never deserted me.

As a very young child I was taken by an old lady, who brought me up in her household among her own grandchildren, and who could scarcely have shown me more kindness had I been one of them. Indeed, I was so spoiled by my kind patroness that, but for being frequently with my mother, I might very likely have grown up idle and useless. But I saw so much of mother, and of her patients, that the ambition to become a doctress early took firm root in my mind.

Then I began to make use of the little knowledge I had acquired from watching my mother, upon a great sufferer — my doll.

I have noticed always what actors children are. If you leave one alone in a room, how soon it clears a little stage and, making an audience out of a few chairs and stools, proceeds to act its childish griefs and blandishments upon its doll. Likewise, I made good use of my dumb companion and confidante, and whatever disease was most prevalent in Kingston, be sure my poor doll soon contracted it. I have had many medical triumphs in later days and saved some valuable lives, but I really think that few have given me more real gratification than the rewarding glow of health which my fancy used to picture stealing over my first patient's toy face after long and precarious illness.

Before long it was very natural that I should seek to extend my practice, and so I found other patients in the dogs and cats around me. Many luckless brutes were made to simulate diseases which were raging among their owners, and had forced down their reluctant throats the remedies which I deemed most likely to suit their supposed complaints. After a time I rose still higher in my ambition and, despairing of finding another human patient, I proceeded to try my simple remedies upon myself.

At twelve years old I was more frequently at my mother's house and used to assist her in her duties, very often sharing with her the task of attending upon invalid officers or their wives, who came to her house from the adjacent camp at Up-Park, or the military station at Newcastle.

As I grew into womanhood I began to indulge that longing to travel which will never leave me while I have health and vigour. I was never weary of tracing upon an old map the route to England, and never followed with my gaze the stately ships homeward bound without longing to be in them and see the blue hills of Jamaica fade into the distance. At that time it seemed improbable that these girlish wishes should be gratified, but circumstances enabled me to accompany some relatives to England while I was yet a very young woman.

I shall never forget my first impressions of London. Of course, I am not going to bore the reader with them, but they are as vivid now as though the year 18— (I very nearly let my age slip then) had not been long ago numbered with the past. Strangely enough, some of the most vivid of my recollections are the efforts of the London streetboys to poke fun at me and my companion's complexion. I am only a little brown — a few shades duskier than the brunettes whom you all admire so much, but my companion was very dark, and a fair (if I can apply the term to her) subject for their rude wit.

She was hot-tempered, poor thing, and as there were no policemen to restrain the boys, our progress through the London streets was sometimes a rather chequered one.

I remained in England, upon the occasion of my first visit, about a year, and then returned to Kingston. Before long I again started for London, bringing with me this time a large stock of West Indian preserves and pickles for sale. After remaining two years, I again started home and, on the way, my life and adventures were very nearly brought to a premature conclusion.

Christmas Day had been kept very merrily on board our ship the *Velusia* and, on the following day, a fire broke out in the hold. I dare say it would have resisted all the crew's efforts to put it out, had not another ship appeared in sight, upon which the fire quietly allowed itself to be distinguished. Although considerably alarmed, I did not lose my senses, but during the time when the contest between fire and water was doubtful, I entered into an amicable arrangement with the ship's cook, whereby, in consideration of two pounds he agreed to lash me on to a large hencoop should I need to jump overboard.

Before I had been long in Jamaica I started upon other trips, many of them undertaken with a view to gain. Thus I

spent some time in New Providence, bringing home with
me a large collection of handsome shells and rare shellwork,
which created quite a sensation in Kingston, and had a rapid
sale. I visited also Haiti and Cuba. But I hasten onward in
my narrative.

Returned to Kingston, I nursed my old indulgent
patroness in her last long illness. After she died in my arms
I went to my mother's house, where I stayed, making myself
useful in a variety of ways, and learning a great deal of
Creole medicinal art, until I couldn't find courage to say
"no" to a certain arrangement timidly proposed by Mr.
Seacole, but married him, and took him down to Black
River, where we established a store.

Poor man! He was very delicate, and before I undertook
the charge of him, several doctors had expressed most
unfavourable opinions of his health. I kept him alive by
kind nursing and attention as long as I could, but at last he
grew so ill that we left Black River, and returned to my
mother's house in Kingston. Within a month of our arrival
there he died.

This was my first great trouble, and I felt it bitterly. For
days I never stirred — not to all that passed around me in a
dull stupor of despair. If you had told me that the time
would soon come when I should remember this sorrow
calmly, I should not have believed it possible. And yet it was
so. I do not think that we hot-blooded Creoles sorrow less
for showing it so impetuously, but I do think that the sharp
edge of our grief wears down sooner than theirs who
preserve an outward demeanour of calmness, and nurse
their woe secretly in their hearts.

CHAPTER 2

I had one other great grief to master — the loss of my mother, and then I was left alone to battle with the world as best I might. The struggles which it cost me to succeed in life were sometimes very trying, nor have they ended yet. But I have always turned a bold front to fortune and taken, and shall continue to take, as my brave friends in the army and navy have shown me how, "my hurts before".

Although it was no easy thing for a widow to make ends meet, I never allowed myself to know what depression was, and so succeeded in gaining not only my daily bread, but many comforts besides from the beginning. Indeed, my experience of the world — it is not finished yet, but I do not think it will give me reason to change my opinion — leads me to the conclusion that it is by no means the hard, bad world which some selfish people would have us believe it. It may be as my editor says, that "gently comes the world to those that are cast in gentle mould." Hinting at the same time, politely, that the rule may apply to me personally.

Perhaps he is right. Although I was always a hearty, strong woman — you might even say stout — I think my heart is soft enough.

How slowly and gradually I succeeded in life. My fortunes underwent the variations which befall all. Sometimes I was rich one day and poor the next. I never thought too exclusively of money, believing rather that we were born to be happy and that the surest way to be wretched is to prize it too much. Had I done so, I should have mourned over many a promising speculation proving a failure, over many a pan of preserves or guava jelly burnt in the making, and perhaps lost my mind when the great fire of 1843, which devastated Kingston, burnt down my poor home. As it was, I very nearly lost my life, for I would not leave my house until every chance of saving it had gone, and it was wrapped in flames.

But, of course, I set to work again in a humbler way, and rebuilt my house by degrees, and restocked it, succeeding better than before, for I had gained a reputation as a skillful nurse and doctress, and my house was always full of invalid officers and their wives from Newcastle, or the adjacent Up-Park Camp. Sometimes I had a naval or military surgeon under my roof, from whom I never failed to glean instruction, given, when they learned my love for their profession, with a readiness and kindness I am never likely to forget. Many of these kind friends are still alive. I met with some when my adventures had carried me to the battlefields of the Crimea, and to those whose eyes may rest upon these pages I again offer my acknowledgments for their past kindness, which helped me to be useful to my kind in many lands.

Here I may take the opportunity of explaining that it was from a confidence in my own powers, and not at all from necessity, that I remained an unprotected female. I do not mind confessing to my reader, in a friendly confidential way, that one of the hardest struggles of my life in Kingston was to resist the pressing candidates for the late Mr. Seacole's shoes.

Officers of high rank sometimes took up their abode in

my house. Others of inferior rank were familiar with me,
long before their bravery and, alas, too often death, in the
Crimea, made them world famous. There were few officers
of the 97th to whom Mother Seacole was not well known,
before she joined them in front of Sebastopol, and among
the best known was good-hearted, loveable, noble H.V.,
whose death shocked me so terribly, and with whose useful
heroic life the English public have become so familiar. I can
hear the ring of his boyish laugh even now.

In the year 1850, the cholera swept over the island of
Jamaica with terrible force. Our idea — perhaps an
unfounded one — was, that a steamer from New Orleans
was the means of introducing it into the island. Anyhow,
they sent some clothes on shore to be washed, and poor
Dolly Johnson, the washerwoman, whom we all knew,
sickened and died of the terrible disease. While the cholera
raged, I had but too many opportunities of watching its
nature, and from a Dr. B, who was then lodging in my
house, received many hints as to its treatment which I
afterwards found invaluable.

Early in the same year my brother had left Kingston for
the Isthmus of Panama, then the great high road to and from
golden California, where he had established a considerable
store and hotel. Ever since he had done so, I had found some
difficulty in checking my reviving disposition to roam, and
at last persuading myself that I might be of use to him (he
was far from strong), I resigned my house into the hands of
a cousin, and made arrangements to journey to Chagres.

Having come to this conclusion, I allowed no grass to
grow beneath my feet, but set to work busily, for I was not
going to him empty-handed. My house was full for weeks,
of tailors, making up rough coats, trousers, etc., and

seamstresses cutting out and making shirts. In addition to these, my kitchen was filled with busy people, manufacturing preserves, guava jelly and other delicacies, while a considerable sum was invested in the purchase of preserved meats, vegetables, and eggs.

It will be as well, perhaps, if I explain, in as few words as possible, the then condition of the Isthmus of Panama.

All my readers must know — a glance at the map will show it to those who do not — that between North America and the envied shores of California stretches a little neck of land, insignificant-looking enough on the map, dividing the Atlantic from the Pacific. By crossing this, the travellers from America avoided a long, weary and dangerous sea voyage round Cape Horn, or an almost impossible journey by land.

But that journey across the Isthmus, insignificant in distance as it was, was by no means an easy one. It seemed as if nature had determined to throw every conceivable obstacle in the way of those who should seek to join the two great oceans of the world. I have read and heard many accounts of old endeavours to effect this important and gigantic work, and how miserably they failed. It was reserved for the men of our age to accomplish what so many had died in attempting, and iron and steam, twin giants, subdued to man's will, have put a girdle over rocks and rivers, so that travellers can glide as smoothly, if not as inexpensively, over the once terrible Isthmus of Darien, as they can from London to Brighton.

Not yet, however, does civilization rule at Panama. The weak sway of the New Granada Republic, despised by lawless men, and respected by none, is powerless to control the refuse of every nation which meet together upon its soil.

Whenever they feel inclined now they overpower the law easily, but seven years ago, when I visited the Isthmus of Panama, things were much worse, and a licence existed, compared to which the present lawless state of affairs is enviable.

When, after passing Chagres, an old world, tumbledown town, for about seven miles, the steamer reached Navy Bay, I thought I had never seen a more luckless, dreary spot. Three sides of the place were a mere swamp, and the town itself stood upon a sandreef, the houses being built upon piles, which someone told me rotted regularly every three years. The railway, which now connects the bay with Panama, was then being built, and ran, as far as we could see, on piles, connected with the town by a wooden jetty. It seemed as capital a nursery for ague and fever as Death could hit upon anywhere, and those on board the steamer who knew it confirmed my opinion.

As we arrived, a steady downpour of rain was falling from an inky sky, the white men who met us on the wharf appeared ghostly and wraith-like, and the very negroes seemed pale and wan. The news which met us did not tempt me to lose any time in getting up the country to my brother. According to all accounts, fever and ague, with some minor diseases, especially dropsy, were having it all their own way at Navy Bay and, although I only stayed one night in the place, my medicine chest was called into requisition.

The sufferers wanted remedies which I could not give them — warmth, nourishment, and fresh air. Beneath leaky tents, damp huts, and even under broken railway wagons, I saw men dying from sheer exhaustion. Indeed, I was very glad when, with the morning, the crowd, as the Yankees called the bands of pilgrims to and from California, made ready to ascend to Panama.

The first stage of our journey was by railway to Gatun, about twelve miles distant. For the greater portion of that distance the lines ran on piles, over as unhealthy and wretched a country as the eye could well grow weary of, but, at last, the country improved, and you caught glimpses of distant hills and English-like scenery.

Every mile of that fatal railway cost the world thousands of lives. I was assured that its site was marked thickly by graves, and that so great was the mortality among the labourers that three times the survivors struck in a body, and their places had to be supplied by fresh victims from America, tempted by unheardof rates of wages. It is a gigantic undertaking, and shows what the energy and enterprise of man can accomplish. Everything requisite for its construction, even the timber, had to be prepared in, and brought from, America.

The railway then ran no further than Gatun, and here we were to take water and ascend the River Chagres to Gorgona, the next stage on the way to Cruces, where my brother was. The cars landed us at the bottom of a somewhat steep cutting through a reddish clay, and deposited me and my entourage, consisting of a black servant, named Mac and a little girl, in safety in the midst of my many packages, not altogether satisfied with my prospects, for the rain was falling heavily and steadily, and the Gatun porters were possessing themselves of my luggage with that same avidity which distinguishes their brethren on the pier of Calais or the quays of Pera. There are two species of individuals whom I have found alike wherever my travels have carried me — the reader can guess their professions — porters and lawyers.

It was as much as I could do to gather my packages together, sit in the midst with a determined look to awe the hungry crowd around me, and send Mac up the steep slippery bank to report progress.

After a little while he returned to say that the riverside was not far off, where boats could be hired for the upward journey. The word given, the porters threw themselves upon my packages, a pitched battle ensued, out of which issued the strongest Spanish Indians, with their hardly-earned prizes, and we commenced the ascent of the clayey bank.

Although the surveyors of the Darien highways had considerately cut steps up the steep incline, they had become worse than useless, so I floundered about terribly, more than once losing my footing altogether. As with that due regard to personal appearance which I have always deemed a duty as well as a pleasure to study, I had, before leaving Navy Bay, attired myself in a delicate light blue dress, a white bonnet prettily trimmed, and an equally chaste shawl, the reader can sympathise with my distress. However, I gained the summit, and after an arduous descent, of a few minutes duration, reached the riverside, in a most piteous plight. My pretty dress, from its contact with the Gatun clay, looked as red as if, in the pursuit of science, I had passed it through a strong solution of acid.

By the waterside I found my travelling companions arguing angrily with the shrewd boatmen, and beating down their fares. Upon collecting my luggage, I found, as I had expected, that the porters had not neglected the glorious opportunity of robbing a woman, and that several articles were missing. Complaints, I knew, would not avail me, and stronger measures seemed hazardous and barely advisable in a lawless, out of the way spot, where 'the simple plan, that they should take who have the power, and they should keep who can', seemed universally practiced, and would very likely have been defended by its practitioners upon principle.

It was not so easy to hire a boat as I had been led to expect. The large crowd had made the boatmen somewhat exorbitant in their demands. There were several reasons why I should engage one for my own exclusive use, instead of sharing one with some of my travelling companions. In the first place, my luggage was somewhat bulky and, in the second place, my experience of travel had not failed to teach me that Americans (even from the Northern States) are always uncomfortable in the company of coloured people, and very often show this feeling in stronger ways than by sour looks and rude words. I think, if I have a prejudice against our cousin across the Atlantic — and I do confess to a little — it is not unreasonable. I have a few shades of deeper brown upon my skin which shows me related — and I am proud of the relationship — to those poor mortals whom you once held enslaved, and whose bodies America still owns. Having this bond, and knowing what slavery is, having seen with my eyes and heard with my ears proof positive enough of its horrors, is it surprising that I should be somewhat impatient of the airs of superiority which many Americans have endeavoured to assume over me? Mind, I am not speaking of all. I have met with some delightful exceptions.

At length I succeeded in hiring a boat for the modest consideration of ten pounds, to carry me and my fortunes to Cruces. My boat was far from uncomfortable. Large and flat-bottomed, with an awning, dirty it must be confessed, beneath which swung a hammock, of which I took immediate possession. By the way, the Central Americans should adopt the hammock as their national badge, but for sheer necessity they would never leave it.

The master of the boat, the padrone, was a fine tall negro, his crew were four common enough specimens of humanity, with a marked disregard of the prejudices of society with respect to clothing. A dirty handkerchief rolled over the head, and a wisp of something, which might have been linen, bound round the loins, formed their attire. Perhaps, however, the thick coating of dirt which covered them kept them warmer than more civilized clothing, besides being indisputably more economical.

The boat was generally propelled by paddles, but when the river was shallow, poles were used to punt us along, as on English rivers, the black padrone, whose superior position was indicated by the use of decent clothing, standing at the helm, gesticulating wildly, and swearing Spanish oaths. Very much shocked, of course, but finding it perfectly useless to remonstrate with him, I swung myself in my hammock and leisurely watched the river scene.

The river Chagres lolled with considerable force, now between low marshy shores, now narrowing between steep, thickly-wooded banks. It was liable, as are all rivers in hilly districts, to sudden and heavy floods, and although the padrone, on leaving Gatun, had pledged his soul to land me at Cruces that night, I had not been long afloat before I saw that he would forfeit his worthless pledge, for the wind rose to a gale, ruffling the river here and there into a little sea, the rain came down in torrents, while the river rose rapidly, bearing down on its swollen stream trunks of trees which it tossed about like a giant in sport, threatening to snag us with its playthings every moment. When we came to a sheltered reach, and found that the little fleet of boats which had preceded us had laid to there, I came to the conclusion that, stiff, tired and hungry, I should have to pass a night upon the river Chagres.

All I could get to eat was guava, which grew wild on the banks, and then I watched the padrone curl his long body up among my luggage, and listened to the crew, who had rolled together at the bottom of the boat, snore as peacefully as if they slept between fair linen sheets, in the purest of calico nightgear, and the most unexceptionable of nightcaps, until somehow I fell into a troubled, dreamy sleep.

At daybreak we were enabled to pursue our journey, and in a short time reached Gorgona. I was glad enough to go on shore, as you may imagine.

Gorgona was a mere temporary town of bamboo and wood houses, hastily erected to serve as a station for the crowd. In the present rainy season, when the river was navigable up to Cruces, the chief part of the population migrated thither, so that Gorgona was almost deserted, and looked indescribably damp, dirty and dull.

With some difficulty I found a bakery and a butcher's shop. The meat was not very tempting, for the Gorgona butchers did not trouble themselves about joints, but cut the flesh into strips about three inches wide, and of various lengths. These were hung upon rails, so that you bought your meat by the yard, and were spared any difficulty in the choice of joint. I cannot say that I was favourably impressed with this novel and simple way of avoiding trouble, but I was far too hungry to be particular and, buying a strip for a quarter of a real, carried it off to Mac to cook.

Late that afternoon, the crew landed me, tired, wretched, and out of temper, upon the miserable wharf of Cruces.

CHAPTER 3

The sympathising reader, who very likely has been laughing heartily at my late troubles, can fancy that I was looking forward with no little pleasurable anticipation to reaching my brother's cheerful home at Cruces. After the long night spent on board the wretched boat in my stiff, clayey dress, and the hours of fasting, the warmth and good cheer of the Independent Hotel could not fail to be acceptable.

My brother met me on the rickety wharf with the kindest welcome in his face, although he did not attempt to conceal a smile at my forlorn appearance and, giving the necessary instructions about my luggage, led the way at once to his house, which was situated at the upper end of the street. A capital site, he said, when the rest of the town was under water — which agreeable variety occurred twice or thrice a year unexpectedly.

On our way, he rather damped my hopes by expressing his fears that he should be unable to provide his sister with the accommodation he could wish. For you see, he said, the crowd from Panama has just come in, meeting your crowd from Navy Bay, and I shouldn't be at all surprised if very many of them have no better bed than the store floors. Despite this warning, I was miserably unprepared for the reception that awaited me.

To be sure, I found Cruces as like Gorgona, in its dampness, dirt, and confusion, as it well could be, but the crowd from the goldfields of California had just arrived, having made the journey from Panama on mules, and the street was filled with motley groups in picturesque variety of attire. The hotels were also full of them, while many lounged in the verandahs after the day's journey. Rude, coarse golddiggers, in gay-coloured shirts, and long, serviceable boots, elbowed, in perfect equality, keen Yankee speculators, as close shaven, neat and clean on the Isthmus of Panama as in the streets of New York or New Orleans. The women alone kept aloof from each other, and well they might, for while a very few seemed not ashamed of their sex, it was somewhat difficult to distinguish the majority from the male companions, save by their bolder and more reckless voice and manner. I must say, however, that many of them adopted male attire for the journey across the Isthmus only, as it spared them many compliments which their husbands were often disposed to resent, however flattering they might be to the choice.

Through all these I pressed on, stiff cold, and hungry, to the Independent Hotel, eagerly anticipating the comforts which awaited me there. At length we reached it. But rest, warmth, comfort — miserable delusions!

Picture a long, low hut, built of rough, unplaned logs, filled with mud and split bamboo, a sloping roof and a large verandah full of visitors. Inside: a long room, gaily hung with dirty calico, in stripes of red and white, above it another room in which the guests slept, having the benefit of sharing in any orgies which might be going on below, through the broad chinks between the rough, irregular planks which formed its floor. At the further end, a small corner, partitioned roughly off, formed a bar, and around it were shelves laden with stores for the travellers, while behind it was a little room used by my brother as his private apartment, but three female travellers had hired it for their own special use for the night, paying the enormous sum of £10 for so exclusive a luxury. At the entrance sat a black man, taking toll of the comers-in, giving them in exchange for coin or gold dust (he had a rusty pair of scales to weigh the latter) a dirty ticket, which guaranteed them supper, a night's lodging and breakfast. I saw all this very quickly, and turned round upon my brother in angry despair.

"What am I to do? Why did you ever bring me to this place? See what a state I am in — cold, hungry and wretched. I want to wash, to change my clothes, to eat."'

Poor Edward could only shrug his shoulders and shake his head in answer to my indignant remonstrances. At last he made room for me in a corner of the crowded bar, set before me some food and left me to watch the strange life I had come to. Before long I soon forgot my troubles in the novelty of my position.

The difference between the passengers to and from California was very distinguishable. Those bound for the gold country were to a certain extent fresh from civilization and had scarcely thrown off its control, whereas the homeward bound revelled in disgusting excess of licence. Although many of the women on their way to California showed clearly enough that the life of licence they sought would not be altogether unfamiliar to them, they still retained some appearance of decency in their attire and manner, but in many cases (as I have before said) the female companions of the successful golddiggers appeared in no hurry to resume the dress or obligations of their sex. Many were clothed as the men were, in shirt and boots, rode their mules in undermine fashion, but with much ease and courage, and in their conversation successfully rivalled the coarseness of their men. I think, on the whole, that those French lady writers who desire to enjoy the privileges of man, with the irresponsibility of the other sex, should have been delighted with the disciples who were carrying their principles into practice in the streets of Cruces.

The chief object of all the travellers seemed to be dinner or supper, I do not know what term they gave it. Down the entire length of the Independent Hotel ran a table covered with a green oilskin cloth and at proper intervals were placed knives and forks, plates and cups and saucers turned down. When a newcomer received his ticket and wished to secure his place for the coming repast, he would turn his plate, cup and saucer up, which mode of reserving seats seemed respected by the rest.

As the evening wore on, the shouting and quarrelling in Yankee twang increased. Some seated themselves at the table and, hammering upon it with the handles of their knives, called out to the excited nigger cooks to make haste with the slapjack. Amidst all this confusion, my brother was quietly selling shirts, boots, trousers, etc., to the travellers, while above all the din could be heard the screaming voices of his touters without drawing attention to the good cheer of the Independent Hotel.

Over and over again, while I cowered in my snug corner, wishing to avoid the notice of all, did I wish myself back in my pleasant home in Kingston, but it was too late now.

At last the table was nearly filled with a motley assemblage of men and women and the slapjack, hot and steaming, was carried in by the black cooks. The hungry diners welcomed its advent with a shout of delight and yet it did not seem particularly tempting. Beyond all doubt it

was a capital *pièce de résistance* for great eaters saw ample
reasons to induce any hotelkeeper to give it his patronage.
In truth, it was a thick substantial pancake of flour, salt and
water — eggs were far too expensive to be used in its
composition and by the time the supply had disappeared, I
thought the largest appetites must have been stayed. But it
was followed by pork, strips of beef stewed with hard
dumplings, hams, great dishes of rice, jugs of molasses and
treacle for sauce, the whole being washed down with an
abundance of tea and coffee. Chickens and eggs were
provided for those who were prepared to pay for these
luxuries of Panama life. So scarce and expensive were they
that, as I afterwards discovered, those hotelkeepers whose
larders were so stocked would hang out a chicken upon
their signposts, as a sure attraction for the richer and more
reckless diggers, while the touter's cry of "Eggs and
chickens here!" was a very telling one. Wine and spirits
were also obtainable, but were seldom taken by the
Americans, who are abstemious abroad as well as at home.

After dinner the store soon cleared. Gambling was a
great attraction, but my brother, dreading its consequences
with these hot-brained armed men, allowed none to take
place in his hotel. So some lounged away to the faro and
monte tables, which were doing a busy trade, others loitered
in the verandah, smoking and looking at the native women,
who sang and danced fandangos before them. The whole of
the dirty, woebegone place, which had looked so wretched
by the light of day, was brilliantly illuminated now. Night
would bring no rest to Cruces, while the crowds were there
to be fed, cheated or amused.

Daybreak would find the faro tables, with their piles of
silver and little heaps of gold dust, still surrounded by

haggard gamblers. Daybreak would gleam sickly upon the tawdry finery of the poor Spanish singers and dancers, whose weary night's work would enable them to live upon the travellers' bounty for the next week or so. These few hours of gaiety and excitement were to provide the Craces people with food and clothing for as many days and, while their transitory sun shone, I will do them the justice to say they gathered in their hay busily.

In the exciting race for gold, we need not be surprised at the strange groups which line the racecourse. All that I wondered at was, that I had not foreseen what I found, or that my rage for change and novelty had closed my ears against the warning voices of those who knew somewhat of the high road to California, but I was too tired to moralise long and begged my brother to find me a bed somewhere. He failed to do so completely and, in despair, I took the matter in my own hands and, stripping the green oilskin cloth from the rough table — it would not be wanted again until tomorrow's breakfast — pinned up some curtains round the table's legs and turned in with my little servant beneath it. It was some comfort to know that my brother, his servants and Mac brought their mattresses and slept near us. It was a novel bed and required some slight stretch of the imagination to fancy it a four-poster, but I was too tired to be particular and slept soundly.

We were up right early on the following morning and, refreshed with my night's sleep, I entered heartily into the preparations for breakfast. That meal over, the homeward bound passengers took boats en route for Gorgona, while those bound for California hired mules for the land journey to Panama. So after a while, all cleared away and Cruces was left to its unhealthy solitude.

CHAPTER 4

I do not think I have ever known what it is to despair, or even to despond (if such were my inclination, I have had some opportunities recently) and it was not long before I began to find out the bright side of Cruces life and enter into schemes for staying there. It would be a week or so before the advent of another crowd would wake Cruces to life and activity again. In the meanwhile, and until I could find a convenient hut for my intended hotel, I remained my brother's guest.

It was destined that I should not be long in Cruces before my medicinal skill and knowledge were put to the test. Before the passengers for Panama had been many days gone, it was found that they had left one of their number behind them and that one was the cholera. I believe that the faculty have not yet come to the conclusion that the cholera is contagious and I am not presumptuous enough to forestall them, but my people have always considered it to be so and the poor Cruces folks did not hesitate to say that this new and terrible plague had been a fellow traveller with the Americans from New Orleans or some other of its favoured haunts.

I had the first intimation of its unwelcome presence in the following abrupt and unpleasant manner:

A Spaniard, an old and intimate friend of my brother, had supped with him one evening and, upon returning home had been taken ill and after a short period of intense suffering had died. So sudden and so mysterious a death gave rise to the rumour that he had been poisoned and suspicion rested for a time, perhaps not unnaturally, upon my brother, in whose company the dead man had last been. Anxious for many reasons — the chief one, perhaps, the position of my brother — I went down to see the corpse. A single glance at the poor fellow showed me the terrible truth. The distressed face, sunken eyes, cramped limbs and discoloured, shrivelled skin were all symptoms which I had been familiar with very recently and at once I pronounced the cause of death to be cholera. The Cruces people were mightily angry with me for expressing such an opinion, even my brother, although it relieved him of the odium of a great crime, was as annoyed as the rest. But by twelve o'clock that morning one of the Spaniard's friends was attacked similarly and the very people who had been most angry with me a few hours previously, came to me now eager for advice.

There was no doctor in Cruces, the nearest approach to one was a little timid dentist, who was there by accident and who refused to prescribe for the sufferer. I was obliged to do my best.

Selecting from my medicine chest — I never travel anywhere without it — what I deemed necessary, I went hastily to the patient and at once adopted the remedies I considered fit. It was a very obstinate case, but by dint of mustard emetics, warm fomentations, mustard plasters on the stomach and the back and calomel, at first in large then in gradually smaller doses, I succeeded in saving my first cholera patient in Cruces.

For a few days the terrible disease made such slow

progress amongst us that we almost hoped it had passed on its way and spared us, but all at once it spread rapidly and afrighted faces, and cries of woe soon showed how fatally the destroyer was at work. In so great request were my services, that for days and nights together I scarcely knew what it was to enjoy two successive hours' rest.

Here I must pause to set myself right with my kind reader. He or she will not, I hope, think that, in narrating these incidents, I am exalting my poor part in them unduly. I do not deny (it is the only thing indeed that I have to be proud of) that I am pleased and gratified when I look back upon my past life and see times now and then and places here and there, when and where I have been enabled to benefit my fellow creatures suffering from ills my skill could often remedy. Nor do I think that the kind reader will consider this feeling an unworthy one. If it be so and if, in the following pages, the account of what Providence has given me strength to do on larger fields of action be considered vain or egotistical, still I cannot help narrating them, for my share in them appears to be the one and only claim I have to interest the public ear. Moreover I shall be sadly disappointed, if those years of life which may be still in store for me are not permitted by Providence to be devoted to similar usefulness. I am not ashamed to confess — for the gratification is, after all, a selfish one — that I love to be of service to those who need a woman's help. And wherever the need arises — on whatever distant shore — I ask no greater or higher privilege than to minister to it. After this explanation, I resume more freely the account of my labours in Cruces.

It was scarcely surprising that the cholera should spread rapidly, for fear is its powerful auxiliary and the Cruces people bowed down before the plague in slavish despair. The Americans and other foreigners in the place showed a brave front, but the natives, constitutionally cowardly, made not the feeblest show of resistance. Beyond filling the poor church and making the priests bring out into the streets figures of tawdry dirty saints, supposed to possess some miraculous influence which they never exerted, before which they prostrated themselves, invoked their aid with passionate prayers and cries, they did nothing. Very likely the saints would have got the credit of helping them if they had helped themselves, but the poor cowards never stirred a finger to clean out their close, reeking huts, or rid the damp streets of the rotting accumulation of months. I think their chief reliance was on " the yellow woman from Jamaica with the cholera medicine." Nor was this surprising, for the Spanish doctor, who was sent for from Panama, became nervous and frightened at the horrors around him and the people soon saw that he was not familiar with the terrible disease he was called upon to do battle with and preferred trusting to one who was.

It must be understood that many of those who could afford to pay for my services did so handsomely, but the great majority of my patients had nothing better to give their doctress than thanks. The best part of my practice lay amongst the American store and hotel keepers, the worst among the native boatmen and muleteers. These latter died by scores and among them I saw some scenes of horror I would fain forget, if it were possible. One terrible night, passed with some of them, has often haunted me. I will endeavour to narrate it and should the reader be supposed to think it highly coloured and doubtful, I will only tell him that, terrible as it seems, I saw almost as fearful scenes on the Crimean peninsula among British men, a few thousand miles only from comfort and plenty.

It was late in the evening when the largest mule owner in Cruces came to me and implored me to accompany him to his *kraal*, a short distance from the town, where he said one of his men was dying. One in particular, his head muleteer, a valuable servant he was most selfishly anxious for, and on the way there promised me a large renumeration if I should succeed in saving him.

Our journey was not a long one but it rained hard and the fields were flooded, so it took us a long time to reach the long, low hut he called 'home'. I would rather not see such another scene as the interior of that hut presented. Its roof scarcely sheltered its wretched inmates from the searching rain, its floor was the damp, rank turf trodden by the mule's hoofs and the muleteers' feet into thick mud. Around, in dirty hammocks and on the damp floor, were the inmates of this wretched place, male and female, the strong and the sick together, breathing air that nearly choked me, accustomed as I had grown to live in impure atmosphere; for beneath the same roof the mules, more valuable to their master than his human servants, were stabled, their fore-feet locked, and beside them were heaps of saddles, packs and harnesses. The groans of the sufferers and the anxiety and fear of their comrades were so painful to hear and witness, that for a few minutes I felt an almost uncontrollable impulse to run out into the stormy night, and flee this plague-spot. But the weak feeling vanished and I set about my duty.

The mule-owner was so frightened that he did not hesitate to obey orders. By my directions, doors and shutters were thrown open, fires were lighted, and every effort made to ventilate the place. Then, with the aid of the frightened women, I applied myself to my poor patients. Two were beyond my skill. Death alone could give them relief. The others I could help. But no words of mine could induce them to bear their terrible sufferings like men. They screamed and groaned, not like women, for few would have been so craven-hearted, but like children; calling, in the intervals of violent pain, upon Jesu, the Madonna, and all the saints of heaven whom their lives had scandalized.

I stayed with them until midnight and then got away for a little time. But I had not long been gone when the mule-master was after me again. The men were worse; would I return with him. The rain was falling heavily on the thatched roof, as it does in tropical climates, and I was tired of death; but I could not resist his appeal. He had brought with him, a pair of tall, thick boots, in which I was to wade through the flooded fields. With some difficulty, I again reached the kraal.

I found the worst cases sinking fast, one of the others had relapsed, while fear had paralyzed the efforts of the rest. I eventually managed to restore some order and, with the help of the bravest women, fixed up screens around the dying men. But no screens could shut out from the others their awful groans and cries for the aid that no mortal power could give them.

So the long night passed away; first a deathlike stillness behind one screen, and then a sudden silence behind another, showing that the fierce battle with death was over, and who had been the victor. Meanwhile, I sat before the flickering fire, with my last patient on my lap, a poor, little brown-faced orphan infant, scarcely a year old, who was dying in my arms and I was powerless to save it. It may

seem strange, but it is a fact that I thought more of that little
child than I did of the men who were struggling for their
lives, and prayed very earnestly and solemnly to God to
spare it. But it did not please Him to grant my prayer, and
towards morning the wee spirit left this sinful world for the
home above it had so lately left and what was mortal of the
little infant lay dead in my arms. Then it was that I began to
think — how the idea first arose in my mind I can hardly say
— that, if it were possible to take this little child and
examine it, I should learn more of the terrible disease which
was sparing neither young nor old and should know better
how to do battle with it. I was not afraid to use my baby
patient thus. I knew its fled spirit would not reproach me,
for I had done all I could for it in life — had shed tears over
it and prayed for it.

It was cold grey dawn and the rain had ceased, when I
followed the man who had taken the dead child away to
bury it and bribed him to carry it by an unfrequented path
down to the riverside and accompany me to the thick retired
bush on the opposite bank. Having persuaded him thus
much, it was not difficult, with the help of silver arguments
to convince him that it would be for the general benefit and
his own, if I could learn from this poor little thing the secret
inner workings of our common foe and ultimately he stayed
by me and aided me in my first and last post mortem
examination. It seems a strange deed to accomplish and I
am sure I could not wield the scalpel or the substitute I then
used now, but at that time the excitement had strung my
mind up to a high pitch of courage and determination and
perhaps the daily, almost hourly, scenes of death had made
me somewhat callous. I need not linger on this scene, nor
give the readers the results of my operation, although novel

to me and decidedly useful, they were what every medical man well knows.

We buried the poor little body beneath a piece of luxuriant turf and stole back into Cruces like guilty things.

The knowledge I had obtained thus strangely was very valuable to me and was soon put into practice. But that I dreaded boring my readers, I would fain give them some idea of my treatment of this terrible disease. I have no doubt that at first I made some lamentable blunders and, maybe, lost patients which a little later I could have saved. I know I came across, the other day, some notes of cholera medicines which made me shudder and I dare say they have been used in their turn and found wanting. The simplest remedies were perhaps the best. Mustard plasters and calomel, the mercury applied externally, where the veins were nearest the surface, were my usual resources. Opium I rather dreaded, as its effect is to incapacitate the system from making any exertion and it lulls the patient into a sleep which is often the sleep of death. When my patients felt thirsty, I would give them water in which cinnamon had been boiled. One stubborn attack succumbed to an additional dose of ten grains of sugar of lead, mixed in a pint of water, given in doses of a tablespoonful every quarter of an hour. Another patient, a girl, I rubbed over with warm oil, camphor and spirits of wine. Above all, I never neglected to apply mustard poultices to the stomach, spine and neck and particularly to keep my patient warm about the region of the heart. Nor did I relax my care when the disease had passed by, for danger did not cease when the great foe was beaten off. The patient was left prostrate, strengthening medicines had to be given cautiously, for fever, often of the brain, would follow. But, after all, one great conclusion, which my practice in cholera cases enabled me to come to, was the old one, that few constitutions permitted the use of exactly similar remedies and that the course of treatment which saved one man, would, if persisted in, have very nearly killed his brother.

Generally speaking, the cholera showed symptoms such as giddiness, sickness, diarrhoea, or sunken and distressed look, but sometimes the substance followed its foreclosing shadow so quickly and the crisis was so rapid, that there was no time to apply any remedies. An American carpenter complained of giddiness and sickness. These warning signs were succeeded so quickly by the worst symptoms of cholera, that in less than an hour his face became an indigo tint and his limbs were doubled up horribly with violent cramps before he died.

To the convicts — and if there could be grades of wretchedness, these poor creatures were the lowest — belonged the terrible task of burying the dead, a duty to which they showed the most repugnance. Not unfrequently, at some fancied alarm, they would fling down their burden, until at last it became necessary to employ soldiers to see that they discharged the task allotted to them. Ordinarily, the victims were buried immediately after death, with such imperfect rites of sepulture as the harassed frightened priests would pay them and very seldom was time afforded by the authorities to the survivors to pay those last offices to the departed which a Spaniard and a Catholic considers so important. Once I was present at a terrible scene in the house of a New Granada grandee, whose pride and poverty justified many of the old Spanish proverbs levelled at his caste.

It was when the cholera was at its height and yet he had

left, perhaps on important business, his wife and family and
gone to Panama for three days. On the day after his
departure, the plague broke out in his house and my
services were required promptly. I found the miserable
household in terrible alarm and yet confining their exertions
to praying to a coarse black priest in a black surplice, who,
kneeling beside the couch of the Spanish lady, was praying
(in his turn) to some favourite saint in Cruces. The sufferer
was a beautiful woman, suffering from a violent attack, with
no one to help her, or even to take from her arms the poor
little child they had allowed her to retain. In her intervals of
comparative freedom from pain, her cries to the Madonna
and her husband were heart-rending to hear.

I had the greatest difficulty to rout the stupid priest and
his stupid worshippers and do what I could for the sufferer.
It was very little and before long the unconscious Spaniard
was a widower. Soon after, the authorities came for the
body. I never saw such passionate anger and despair as were
shown by her relatives and servants, old and young, at the
intrusion. Rage that she, who had been so exalted in life,
should go to her grave like the poor, poor clay she was.

Orders were given to bar the door against the convict
gang who had come to discharge their unpleasant duty and,
while all were busy decking out the unconscious corpse in
gayest attire, none paid any heed to me bending over the fire
with the motherless child, journeying fast to join its dead
parent. I had made more than one effort to escape, for I felt
more sick and wretched than at any similar scene of woe,
but finding exit impossible, I turned my back upon them
and attended to the dying child. Nor did I heed their actions
until I heard orders given to admit the burial party and then
I found that they had dressed the corpse in white satin and

decked her head with flowers.

The agitation and excitement of this scene had greeted me as no previous horror had done and I could not help fancying that symptoms were showing themselves in me with which I was familiar enough in others. Leaving the dying infant to the care of its relatives (when the Spaniard returned he found himself widowed and childless), I hastened to my brother's house. When there, I felt an unpleasant chill come over me and went to bed at once. Other symptoms followed quickly and, before nightfall, I knew full well that my turn had come at last and that the cholera had attacked me, perhaps its greatest foe in Cruces.

CHAPTER 5

When it became known that their "yellow doctress" had the cholera, I must do the people of Cruces the justice to say that they gave her plenty of sympathy and would have shown their regard for her more actively had there been any occasion. Indeed, when I most wanted quiet, it was difficult to keep out the sympathising Americans and sorrowing natives who came to inquire after me and who, not content with making their inquiries and leaving their offerings of blankets, flannels etc., must see with their own eyes what chance the yellow woman had of recovery. The rickety door in my little room could never be kept shut for many minutes together. A visitor would open it silently, poke his long face in with an expression of sympathy that almost made me laugh in spite of my pain, draw it out again, between the narrowest possible opening, as if he were anxious to admit as little air as he could, while another would come in boldly and, after looking at me curiously and inquisitively, as he would eye a horse or nigger he had some thoughts of making a bid for, would help to carpet my room, with the result perhaps of his meditations and saying, gravely, "Are you better, Aunty Seacole? Isn't there a something we can do for you, ma'am?" would as gravely give place to another and another yet, until I was almost inclined to throw something at them, or call them bad names. Fortunately, the attack was a very mild one and by the next day all danger had gone by, although I still felt weak and exhausted.

After a few weeks, the first force of the cholera was spent and, although it lingered with us, as though loath to leave so fine a resting place for some months, it no longer gave us much alarm. Before long, life went on as briskly and selfishly as ever with the Cruces survivors and the terrible past was conveniently forgotten.

Perhaps it is so everywhere, but the haste with which the Cruces people buried their memory seemed indecent. Old houses found new masters, the mules new drivers, the great Spaniard chose another pretty woman and had a grand, poor, dirty wedding and was married by the same lazy black priest who had buried his wife a few months back and very likely they would all have hastened as quickly to forget their doctress, had circumstances permitted them. But every now and then one of them sickened and died of the old complaint and the reputation I had established founded for me a considerable practice. The Americans in the place gladly retained me as their medical attendant and, in one way or other, gave me plenty to do. In addition to this, I determined to follow my original scheme of keeping a hotel in Cruces.

Right opposite my brother's Independent Hotel there was a place to let, which it was considered I could adapt to my purpose. It was a mere tumbledown hut with a rotten thatched roof, containing two rooms, one small enough to serve as a bedroom. For this charming residence — very openly situated and well ventilated — twenty pounds a month was considered a fair and by no means exorbitant rent.

I was glad to take possession of it and in a few days had hung its bare walls with calico of the gayest colour in stripes, with an exuberance of fringes, frills and bows (the Americans love show dearly) and prepared it to accommodate fifty dinner guests. I had determined that it should be simply an eating house and that I would receive no lodgers. Once and once only, I relaxed this rule in favour of two American women, who sent me to sleep by a lengthy quarrel of words, woke me in the night to witness its crisis in a fisticuff duel and left in the morning, after having taken a fancy to some of my moveables which were most easily removable.

I had on my staff my black servant Mac, the little girl I have before alluded to and a native cook. I had had many opportunities of seeing how my brother conducted his business and adopted his tariff of charges. For an ordinary dinner my charge was four shillings. Eggs and chickens were, as I have before said, distinct luxuries and fetched higher prices.

Four crowds generally passed through Cruces every month. In these were to be found passengers to and from Chile, Peru and Lima, as well as California and America. The distance from Cruces to Panama was not great. Only twenty miles, in fact, but the journey, from the want of roads and the roughness of the country, was a most fatiguing one. In some parts, as I found when I made the journey in company with my brother, it was almost impassable and for more than half the distance, three miles an hour was considered splendid progress. The great majority of the travellers were rough, rude men, of dirty, quarrelsome habits, the others were more civilized and more dangerous.

It was not long before I grew very tired of life in Cruces, although I made money rapidly and pressed my brother to return to Kingston. Poor fellow, it would have been well for him had he done so, for he stayed only to find a grave on the Isthmus of Panama.

The company at my eating house was not over select and it was often very difficult for an unprotected female to manage them, although I always did my best to put them in good humour. Among other comforts, I used to hire a black barber, for the rather large consideration of two pounds, to shave my male guests. You can scarcely conceive the pleasure and comfort an American feels in a clean chin and I believe my barber attracted considerable custom to the British Hotel at Cruces. I had a little outhouse erected for his special convenience and there, well provided with towels and armed with plenty of razors, a brush of extraordinary size and a foaming sea of lather, José shaved the newcomers. The rivalry to get within reach of his huge brush was very great and the threats used by the neglected, when the grinning black man was considered guilty of any interested partiality, were of the fiercest description.

This duty over, they and their coarser female companions — many of them well known to us, for they travelled backwards and forwards across the Isthmus, hanging on to the foolish goldfinders — attacked the dinner, very often with great lack of decency. It was no use giving them carving knives and forks, for very often they laid them down to insert a dirty hairy hand into a full dish, while the floor soon bore evidences of the great national American habit of expectoration. Very often quarrels would arise during the progress of dinner and more than once I thought their knives would have been turned against one another. It was, I always thought, extremely fortunate that the reckless men rarely stimulated their excitable passions with strong drink. Tea and coffee were the common beverages of the

Americans, Englishmen and men of other nations, being generally distinguishable by their demand for wine and spirits. But the Yankee's capacity for swilling tea and coffee was prodigious. I saw one man drink ten cups of coffee and finding his appetite still unsatisfied, I ran across to my brother for advice. There was a merry twinkle in his eyes as he whispered, "I always put in a good spoonful of salt after the sixth cup. It chokes them off admirably."

It was no easy thing to avoid being robbed and cheated by the less scrupulous travellers, although I think it was only the smartest Yankee who stood any fair chance of out-witting me. I remember an instance which I will narrate, hoping it may make my reader laugh as heartily as its recollection makes me.

He was a tall, thin Yankee, with a furtive glance of the eyes and an amazing appetite, which he seemed nothing loath to indulge. His appetite for eggs especially seemed unbounded. Now, I have more than once said how expensive eggs were and this day they happened to be eight pence apiece. Our plan was to charge every diner according to the number of shells found upon his plate. Now, I noticed how eagerly my thin guest attacked my eggs and marvelled somewhat at the scanty pile of shells before him. My suspicions once excited, I soon fathomed my Yankee friend's dodge. As soon as he had devoured the eggs, he conveyed furtively the shells beneath the table and distributed them impartially at the feet of his companions. I gave my little black maid a piece of chalk and instructions and, creeping under the table, she counted the scattered shells and chalked the number on the tail of his coat. When he came up to pay his score, he gave up his number of eggs in a loud voice. When I contradicted him and referred to the coat-tail in corroboration of my score, there was a general laugh against him. But there was a nasty expression in his cat-like eyes and an unpleasant allusion to mine, which were not agreeable and dissuaded me from playing any more practical jokes upon the Yankees.

I followed my brother's example closely and forbade all gambling in my hotel. Put I got some idea of its fruits from the cases brought to me for surgical treatment from the faro and monte tables. Gambling at Cruces and on the Isthmus generally, was a business by which money was wormed out of the goldseekers and goldfinders. No attempt was made to render it attractive, as I have seen done elsewhere. The gambling house was often plainer than our hotels and but for the green tables, with their piles of money and gold dust, watched over by a well-armed determined banker and the eager gamblers around, you would not know that you were in the vicinity of a spot which the English at home designate by a very decided and extreme name. A Dr. Casey — everybody familiar with the Americans knows their fondness for titles — owned the most favoured table in Cruces, despite being known to be a reckless and unscrupulous villain. Most of them knew that he had been hunted out of San Francisco and, at that time, a man too bad for that city must have been a prodigy of crime. Moreover he was violent-tempered and had a knack of referring the slightest dispute to his revolver. Yet his table was always crowded, probably because — the greatest rogues have some good qualities — he was honest in his way and played fairly.

Occasionally some distinguished passengers passed on the upward and downward tides of rascality and ruffianism, that swept periodically through Cruces.

Came one day, Lola Montes, in the full zenith of her evil fame, bound for California. A good-looking, bold woman, with fine, bad eyes and a determined bearing, dressed ostentatiously in perfect male attire, with shirt collar turned down over a velvet lapelled coat, richly worked shirt-front, black hat, French unmentionables and natty, polished boots with spurs. She carried in her hand a handsome riding whip, which she could use as well in the streets of Cruces as in the towns of Europe. Now an impertinent American, presuming — perhaps not unnaturally — upon her reputation, laid hold jestingly to the tails of her long coat and, as a lesson, received a cut across his face that must have marked him for some days. I did not wait to see the row that followed and was glad when the wretched woman rode off the following morning.

A very different notoriety followed her at some interval of time.

Miss Catherine Bayes, on her successful singing tour, who disappointed us all by refusing to sing at Cruces.

After her came an English bishop from Australia, who need have been a member of the church militia to secure his pretty wife from the host of admirers she had gained during her day's journey from Panama.

Very quarrelsome were the majority of the crowds, holding life cheap, as all bad men strangely do — equally prepared to take or lose it upon the slightest provocation. Few tales of horror in Panama could be questioned on the ground of improbability. Not less partial were many of the natives of Cruces to the use of the knife, preferring, by the way, to administer sly stabs in the back, when no one was by to see the dastard blow dealt.

Terribly bullied by the Americans were the boatmen and

muleteers, who were reviled, shot and stabbed by these free and independent filibusters who would fain whip all creation abroad as they do their slaves at home.

Whenever any Englishmen were present and in a position to interfere with success, this bullying was checked and they found, instead of the poor Spanish Indians, men worthy of their steel or lead. I must do them credit to say, that they were never loath to fight anyone that desired that passing excitement, and thought little of ending their journey of life abruptly at the wretched wayside town of Cruces. It very often happened so and over many a hasty head and ready hand have I seen their hot hearts stilled suddenly in some senseless quarrel. And so in time I grew to have some considerable experience in the treatment of knife and gunshot wounds.

One night I heard a great noise outside my window and, on rising, found a poor boatman moaning piteously and, in a strange jumble of many languages, begging me to help him. At first I was afraid to open the door, on account of the noisy mob which soon joined him, for villainy was very shrewd at Cruces, but at last I admitted him and found that the poor wretch's ears had been cruelly split by some hasty citizen of the United States. I stitched them up as well as I could and silenced his cries.

At any time, if you happened to be near the river when a crowd were arriving or departing, your ears would be regaled with a choice chorus of threats, of which ear-splitting, eye gouging, cowhiding and the application of revolvers were the mildest. Against the negroes, of whom there were many in the Isthmus and who almost invariably filled the municipal offices and took the lead in every way, the Yankees had a strong prejudice, but it was wonderful to see how freedom and equality elevate men and the same negro who perhaps in Tennessee would have cowered like a beaten child or dog, beneath an American's uplifted hand, would face him boldly here and by equal courage and superior physical strength cower his old oppressor.

When more than ordinary squabbles occurred in the street or at the gambling tables, the assistance of the soldier-police of New Granada was called in and the affair sometimes assumed the character of a regular skirmish. The soldiers — I wish I could speak better of them — were a dirty, cowardly, indolent set, more prone to using their knives than their legitimate arms and bore old rusty muskets and very often marched unshod. Their officers were in outward appearance a few shades superior to the men they commanded, but as respects military proficiency, were their equals. Add to this description of their personnel the well-known fact that you might commit the grossest injustice and could obtain the simplest justice simply by lavish bribery, and you may form some idea of our military protectors.

Very practiced and skillful in thieving were the native population of Cruces — I speak of the majority except the negroes — always more inclined to do a dishonest night's labour at great risk, than an honest day's work for fair wages, for justice was always administered strictly to the poor natives — it was only the foreigners who could evade it or purchase exemption. Punishment was severe and, in extreme cases, the convicts were sent to Carthagena, there to suffer imprisonment of a terrible character. Indeed, from what I heard of the New Granada prisons, I thought no other country could match them and continued to think so until I read how the ingenuity in cruelty of His Majesty the

King of Naples put the torturers of the New Granada Republic to the blush.

I generally avoided claiming the protection of the law whilst on the Isthmus, for I found it was — as is the case in civilized England from other causes — rather an expensive luxury. Once only I took a thief caught in the act before the alcalde and claimed the administration of justice.

The courthouse was a low bamboo shed, before which some dirty Spanish-Indian soldiers were lounging. Inside, the alcalde, a negro, was reclining in a dirty hammock, smoking coolly, hearing evidence and pronouncing judgment upon the wretched culprits who were trembling before his dusky majesty. I had attended him while suffering from an attack of cholera and directly he saw me he rose from his hammock and received me in a ceremonious, grand manner and gave orders that coffee should be brought to me. He had a very pretty white wife, who joined us and then the alcalde politely offered me a cigarito — having declined which, he listened to my statement with great attention.

All this, however, did not prevent my leaving the necessary fee in furtherance of justice, nor his accepting it. Its consequence was that the thief, instead of being punished as a criminal, was ordered to pay me the value of the stolen goods, which, after weeks of hesitation and delay, she eventually did, in pearls, combs and other curiosities.

Whenever an American was arrested by the New Granada authorities, justice had a hard struggle for the mastery and rarely obtained it. Once I was present at the courthouse, when an American was brought in heavily ironed, charged with having committed a highway robbery — if I may use the term where there were no roads — of some travellers from Chile. Around the frightened soldiers swelled an angry crowd of brother Americans, abusing and threatening the authorities in no measured terms, all of them indignant that a nigger should presume to judge one of their countrymen. At last their violence so roused the sleepy alcalde, that he positively threw himself from his hammock, laid down his cigarito and gave such very determined orders to his soldiers that he succeeded in checking the riot. Then, with an air of decision that puzzled everybody, he addressed the crowd, declaring angrily that since the Americans came, the country had known no peace, that robberies and crimes of every sort had increased, and ending by expressing his determination to make strangers respect the laws of the Republic and to retain the prisoner and if found guilty, punish him as he deserved. The Americans seemed too astonished at the audacity of the black man who dared thus to beard them, to offer any resistance, but I believe that the prisoner was allowed ultimately to escape.

I once had a narrow escape from the thieves of Cruces. I had been down to Chagres for some stores and, returning late in the evening, too tired to put away my packages, had retired to rest at once. My little maid, who was not so fatigued as I was and slept more lightly, woke me in the night to listen to a noise in the thatch, at the further end of the store, but I was so accustomed to hear the half-starved mules of Cruces munching my thatch, that I listened lazily for a few minutes and then went unsuspiciously into another heavy sleep. I do not know how long it was before I was again awakened by the child's loud screams and cries of "Hombro — landro!" Sure enough, by the light of the dying fire, I saw a fellow stealing away with my dress, in the pocket of which was my purse. I was about to rush forward, when the fire gleamed on a villainous-looking knife in his hand, so I stood still and screamed loudly, hoping to arouse my brother over the way. For a moment the thief seemed inclined to silence me and had taken a few steps forward, when I took up an old rusty horsepistol which my brother had given me that I might look determined, and snatching down the can of ground coffee, proceeded to prime it, still screaming as loudly as my strong lungs would permit, until the rascal turned tail and stole away through the roof. The thieves usually buried their spoil like dogs, as they were, but this fellow had only time to hide it behind a bush, where it was found on the following morning and claimed by me.

CHAPTER 6.

I remained at Cruces until the rainy months came to an end
and the river grew too shallow to be navigable by the boats
higher up than Gorgona. Then we all made preparations for
a flitting to that place. But before starting, it appeared to be
the custom for the store and hotel keepers to exchange
parting visits and to many of these parties I, in virtue of my
recent services to the community, received invitations. The
most important social meeting took place on the
anniversary of the declaration of American independence,
at my brother's hotel, where a score of zealous Americans
dined most heartily — as they never fail to do.

As it was a special occasion, they drank champagne
liberally at twelve shillings a bottle. And, after the usual
patriotic toasts had been duly honoured, they proposed "the
ladies", with a special reference to myself, in a speech which
I thought worth noting down at the time. The spokesman
was a thin, sallow-looking American, with a pompous and
yet rapid delivery and a habit of turning over his words
with his quid before delivering them and clearing his mouth
after each sentence, perhaps to make room for the next.

I shall beg the reader to consider that the blanks express
the time expended on this operation. He dashed into his
work at once, rolling up and getting rid of his sentences as
he went on:

"Well, gentlemen, I expect you'll all support me in a

drinking of this toast that I do — Aunty Seacole, gentlemen, I give you, Aunty Seacole — We can't do less for her, after what she done for us when the cholera was among us, gentlemen, not many months ago —

"So, I say, God bless the best yaller woman He ever made from Jamaica, gentlemen, from the Isle of Springs —

"Well, gentlemen, I expect there are only two things we're vexed for and the first is, that she ain't one of us, a citizen of the great United States, and the other thing is, gentlemen, that Providence made her a yaller woman. I calculate, gentlemen, you're all as vexed as I am that she's not wholly white, but I do reckon on your rejoicing with me that she's so many shades removed from being entirely black and, I guess, if wee could bleach her by any means we would and thus make her as acceptable in any company as she deserves to be —

"Gentlemen, I give you — Aunty Seacole!"

And so the orator sat down amidst much applause. It may be supposed that I did not need much persuasion to return thanks, burning as I was to tell them my mind on the subject of my colour. Indeed, if my brother had not checked me, I should have given them my thoughts somewhat too freely. As it was, I said:

"Gentlemen, I return you my best thanks for your kindness in drinking my health. As for what I have done in Cruces, Providence evidently made me to be useful, I can't help it. But, I must say, that I don't altogether appreciate your friend's kind wishes with respect to my complexion. If it had been as dark as any nigger's, I should have been just as happy and as useful and as much respected by those whose respect I value and as to his offer of bleaching me, I should, even if it were practicable, decline it without any thanks. As to the society which the process might gain me admission into, all I can say is that, judging from the specimens I have met with here and elsewhere, I don't think that I shall lose much by being excluded from it. So, gentlemen, I drink to you and the general reformation of American manners."

I do not think that they altogether admired my speech, but I was a somewhat privileged person and they laughed at it good-naturedly enough. Perhaps (for I was not in the best humour myself) I should have been better pleased if they had been angry.

Rightly, I ought to have gone down to Gorgona a few weeks before Cruces was deserted and secured a hotel, but I did not give up all hope of persuading my brother to leave the Isthmus until the very last moment and then, of course, a suitable house could not be hired in Gorgona for love or money. Seeing his fixed determination to stay, I consented to remain with him, for he was young and often ill and set hard to work to settle myself somewhere.

With the aid of an old Jamaica friend, who had settled at Gorgona, I at last found a miserable little hut for sale and bought it for a hundred dollars. It consisted of one room only and was, in its then condition, utterly unfit for my purpose, but I determined to set to work and build on to it — by no means the hazardous speculation in Gorgona, where bricks and mortar are unknown, that it is in England. The alcalde's permission to make use of the adjacent ground was obtained for a moderate consideration and plenty of material was procurable from the opposite bank of the river. An American, whom I had cured of the cholera at Cruces, lent me his boat and I hired two or three natives to cut down and shape the posts and bamboo poles. Directly these were raised, Mac and my little maid set to work and filled up the spaces between them with split bamboo canes and reeds.

Before long my new hotel was ready to be roofed. The building process was simple enough and I soon found myself in possession of a capital dining room some thirty feet in length, which was gaily hung with coloured calico, concealing all defects of construction and lighted with large oil lamps, a storeroom bar and a small private apartment for ladies. Altogether, although I had to pay my labourers four shillings a day, the whole building did not cost me more than my brother paid for three months' rent of his hotel.

I gave the travelling world to understand that I intended to devote my establishment principally to the entertainment of and the care of those who might fall ill on the route and I found the scheme answer admirably. And yet, although the speculation paid well, I soon grew as weary of my life in Gorgona as I had been at Cruces and, when I found my brother proof against all persuasion to quit the Isthmus, I began to entertain serious thoughts of leaving him.

Nor was it altogether my old roving inclination which led me to desire a change, although I dare say it had something to do with it. My present life was not agreeable for a woman with the least delicacy or refinement, and of female society I had none. Indeed, the females who crossed my path were about as unpleasant specimens of the fair sex as one could well wish to avoid. With very few exceptions, those who were not bad were very disagreeable and, as the majority came from the Southern States of America and showed an instinctive repugnance against anyone whose countenance claimed for her kindred with their slaves, my position was far from a pleasant one. Not that it ever gave me any annoyance, they were glad of my stores and comforts, I made money out of their wants, nor do I think our bond of connection was ever closer. Only this, if any of them came to me sick and suffering (I say this out of simple justice to myself), I forgot everything, except that she was my sister and that it was my duty to help her.

I may have before said that the citizens of the New Granada Republic had a strong prejudice against all Americans. It is not difficult to assign a cause for this. In the first place, many of the negroes, fugitive from the Southern States, had sought refuge in this and the other States of Central America, where every profession was open to them, and as they were generally superior men — evinced perhaps by their hatred of their old condition and their successful flight — they soon rose to positions of eminence in New Granada. In the priesthood, in the army, in all municipal offices, the self-liberated negroes were invariably found in the foremost rank and the people, for some reason — perhaps because they recognised in them superior talents for administration — always respected them more than and preferred them to, their native rulers. So that, influenced naturally by these freed slaves, who bore themselves before their old masters bravely and like men, the New Granada people were strongly prejudiced against the Americans. And in the second and third places, they feared their quarrelsome, bullying habits — be it remembered that the crowds to California were of the lowest sorts, many of whom have since fertilised Cuban and Nicaraguan soil — and dreaded their schemes for annexation. To such an extent was this amusingly carried, that when the American Railway Company took possession of Navy Bay and christened it Aspinwall, after the name of their Chairman, the native authorities refused to recognise their right to name any portion of the Republic and pertinaciously returned all letters directed to Aspinwall, with *'no such place known'* marked upon them in the very spot for which they were intended. And, in addition to this, the legal authorities refused to compel any defendant to appear who was described as of Aspinwall and put every plaintiff out of court who described himself as residing in that unrecognised place.

Under these circumstances, my readers can easily understand that when any Americans crossed the Isthmus, accompanied by their slaves, the Cruces and Gorgona people were restless and anxious to whisper into their ears offers of freedom and hints on how easy escape would be. Nor were the authorities at all inclined to aid in the recapture of a runaway slave. So that, as it was necessary for the losers to go on with the crowd, the fugitive invariably escaped. It is one of the maxims of the New Granada constitution — as it is, I believe, of the English — that on a slave touching its soil his chains fall from him. Rather than irritate so dangerous a neighbour as America, this rule was rarely supported, but I remember the following instance of its successful application.

A young American woman, whose character can be best described by the word 'vicious', fell ill at Gorgona and was left behind by her companions under the charge of a young negro girl, her slave, whom she treated most inhumanly, as was evinced by the poor girl's frequent screams when under the lash. One night her cries were so distressing that Gorgona could stand it no longer, but broke into the house and found the chattel bound hand and foot, naked and being severely lashed. Despite the threats and astonishment of the mistress, they were both carried off on the following

morning, before the alcalde, himself a man of colour and of
a very humane disposition. When the particulars of the case
were laid before him, he became strongly excited and called
upon the woman to offer an explanation of her cruelty. She
treated it with the coolest concern: The girl was her
property, worth so many dollars; had misbehaved herself
and been properly corrected. The alcalde must be drunk or
a fool, or both together, to interfere between an America and
her property, she concluded coolly.

Her coolness vanished, however, when the alcalde
turned round to the girl and told her that she was free to
leave her mistress when she liked. When she heard the
irrepressible cheering of the crowded courthut at the
alcalde's humanity and boldness and saw the slave's face
flush with delight at the judge's words, the American
woman became terribly enraged, made use of the most
fearful threats and would have wreaked summary
vengeance on her late chattel had not the clumsy soldiers
interfered.

Then, with demonic refinement of cruelty, she reminded
herself of the girl's baby at New Orleans, still in her power,
and threatened most horrible torture to the child if its
mother dared to accept the judge's offer.

The poor girl trembled and covered her face with her
hands, as though to shut out some fearful sight and, I think,
had we not persuaded her to the contrary, that she would
have sacrificed her newly-won freedom for the child's sake.
But we knew very well that when the heat of passion had
subsided, the threatener would not injure her own property
and at once set afloat a subscription for the purchase of the
child.

How the tale ended I do not know, as the woman was

very properly removed into the interior of the country.

Life at Gorgona resembled life at Cruces so nearly that it does not need a separate description. Down with the store and hotel keepers came the muleteers and mules, porters and hangers-on, idlers and thieves, gamblers and dancing women and soon the monte tables were fitted up and plying their deadly trade and the dancers charmed the susceptible travellers as successfully in the dirty streets of Gorgona as they had previously done in the unwholesome precincts of Cruces. Dr. Casey was very nearly getting himself into serious trouble, from too great a readiness to use his revolver. Still, he had a better excuse for bloodshed this time than might have been found for his previous breaches of the sixth commandment. Among the desperadoes who frequented his gambling hut, during their short stay in Gorgona, was conceived the desperate plan of shooting out the lights and upsetting Casey's table, trusting in the confusion to carry off the piles of money upon it. The first part of their programme was successfully carried out, but the second was frustrated by the Doctor promptly firing his revolver into the dark and hitting an unoffending boy in the hip. At this point the Gorgona police entered, carried off all the parties they could lay hands upon (including the Doctor) to prison and brought the wounded boy to me.

On the following morning came a most urgent request that I should visit the imprisoned Doctor. I found him desperately angry, but somewhat nervous too, for the alcalde was known to be no friend to the Americans, owed Casey more than one grudge, and had shown recently a disposition to enforce the laws.

"I say, Mrs. Seacole, how's that boy?"

"Oh, Dr. Casey, how could you shoot the poor lad and

now call him bad names, as though he'd injured you? He is very ill indeed — may die, so I advise you to think seriously of your position."

"But Madame Seacole," (this in a very altered tone) "you'll surely help me? You'll surely tell the alcalde that the wound's a slight one? He's a friend of yours and will let me out of this hole. Come, Madame Seacole, you'll never leave me to be murdered by these bloodthirsty savages?"

"What can I do or say, Dr. Casey? I must speak the truth and the ball is still in the poor lad's hip," I answered, for I enjoyed the fellow's fear too much to help him.

However, he sent some of his friends to the boy's father and bribed him to take the lad from my care and send him to Navy Bay, to a surgeon there. Of course, he never returned to prosecute Dr. Casey, who was left with the alcalde only to deal with. Although he hated the man, the alcalde could not resist his money and so set him free.

Gorgona, lying lower than Cruces, its inhabitants more frequently enjoyed the excitement of a flood. After heavy rains the river would rise so rapidly that in a few hours the chief part of the place would be under water. On such occasions the scene was unusually exciting. As the water crept up the street, the frightened householders kept removing their goods and furniture to higher ground, while here and there, where the waters had surrounded them unawares, boats were sent to their rescue. The houses, not made to resist much wind or water, often gave way and were carried down the Chagres. Meanwhile, the thieves were the busiest — the honest folks, forgetting the true old adage, *God helps those who help themselves,* confining their exertions to bringing down their favourite saints to the water's edge and invoking their interposition.

Fortunately my hotel was at the upper end of the town, where the floods had been rarely known to extend and, although there was a sufficient chance of the water reaching me to compel me to have all my stores ready packed for removal, I escaped. Some distressing losses occurred. A Frenchman, a near neighbour, whose house was surrounded by the waters before he could remove his goods, grew so frantic at the loss, that he obstinately refused to quit his falling house and some force had to be used before they could save his life.

Scarcely had the ravages of the last flood been repaired than fire marked Gorgona for its prey.

It began at a store by the riverside, but it spread rapidly. Before long all Gorgona was in danger. The town happened to be packed that night, two crowds having met there, and there was great confusion. Eventually, the lazy soldier-police, aided by the Americans, succeeded in pulling down some old crazy huts and checking the fire's progress. The travellers were in sore plight, many of them being reduced to sleep on their luggage, piled in the drenched streets. My hotel had some interesting inmates, for a poor young creature, borne in from one of the burning houses, became a mother during the night and a stout little lassie opened its eyes upon this awesome world during the excitement and danger of a Gorgona fire.

Shortly after this, tired to death of life in Panama, I handed over my hotel to my brother and returned to Kingston. On the way thither I experienced another instance of American politeness, which I cannot help recording, first reminding my readers of what I have previously said of the character of the Californian travellers. Anxious to get home quickly, I took my passage in the first steamer that left Navy

Bay — an American one.

Late in the evening, I said farewell to the friends I had been staying with and went on board. A very kind friend, an American merchant, doing a large business at Navy Bay, had tried hard to persuade me to delay my journey until the English company's steamer called, without, however, giving any good reasons for his wish. So, with Mac and my little maid, I passed through the crowd of female passengers on deck and sought the privacy of the saloon. :Before I had been long there, two ladies came to me and in their cool, straightforward manner, questioned me.

"Where are you going?"

"To Kingston," I replied.

"And how are you going?"

"By sea."

"Don't be impertinent, yaller woman. By what conveyance are you going?"

"By this steamer, of course. I've paid for my passage."

They went away with this information and in a short time eight or nine others came and surrounded me, asking the same questions. My answers raised quite a storm of uncomplimentary remarks.

"Guess a nigger woman don't go along with us in this saloon," said one.

"I never travelled with a nigger yet and I expect I shan't begin now," said another, while some children had taken my little servant Mary in hand and were practising on her the politeness which their parents were favouring me with — only, as is the wont of children, they were more cruel. I cannot help it if I shock my readers, but the truth is that one positively spat in poor little Mary's frightened yellow face.

At last an old American lady came to where I sat and

gave me some staid advice.

"Well, now, I tell you for your good, you'd better quit this and not drive my people to extremities. If you do, you'll be sorry for it, I expect."

Thus harassed, I appealed to the stewardess — a tall, sour-looking woman, flat and thin as a dressed up broomstick. She asked me sundry questions as to how and when I had taken my passage, until, tired beyond all endurance, I said, "My good woman, put me anywhere — under a boat, in your storeroom — so that I can get to Kingston somehow."

But the stewardess was not to be moved.

"There's nowhere but the saloon, and you can't expect to stay with the white people, that's clear. Flesh and blood can stand a good deal of aggravation, but not that. If the Britishers is so took up with coloured people, that's their business, but it won't do here."

This last remark was in answer to an Englishman, whose advice to me was not to leave my seat for any of them. He made matters worse until at last I lost my temper. Calling Mac, I bade him get my things together and went up to the captain, a good honest man. He and some of the black crew and the black cook, who showed his teeth most viciously, were much annoyed. Muttering about its being a custom of the country, the captain gave me an order upon the agent for the money I had paid and so, at twelve o'clock at night, I was landed again upon the wharf of Navy Bay.

My American friends were vastly annoyed, but not much surprised. Two days later, the English steamer, the *Eagle*, in charge of my old friend, Captain B. docked at Navy Bay and carried me to Kingston.

CHAPTER 7

I stayed in Jamaica eight months out of the year 1853, still remembered in the island for its suffering and gloom. I returned just in time to find my services, with many others, needful, for the yellow fever never made a more determined effort to exterminate the English in Jamaica than it did in that dreadful year.

So violent was the epidemic, that some of my people fell victims to its fury, a thing rarely heard of before. My house was full of sufferers — officers, their wives and children. Very often they were borne in from the ships in the harbour, sometimes in a dying state, sometimes — after long and distressing struggles with the grim foe — to recover. Habituated as I had become with death in its most harrowing forms, I found these scenes more difficult to bear than any I had previously borne a part in and for this reason perhaps, that I had not only to cheer the deathbed of the sufferer, but, far more trying task, to soothe the passionate grief of wife or husband left behind. It was a terrible thing to the young people in the youth and bloom of life suddenly stricken down, not in battle with an enemy that threatened their country, but in vain contest with a climate that refused to adopt them. Indeed, the mother country pays a dear price for the possession of her colonies.

I think all who are familiar with the West Indies will acknowledge that Nature has been favourable to strangers in a few respects and that one of these has been in instilling into the hearts of the Creoles an affection for English people and an anxiety for their welfare, which shows itself warmest when they are sick and suffering. I can safely appeal on this point to anyone who is acquainted with life in Jamaica. Another benefit has been conferred upon them by inclining the Creoles to practice the healing art and inducing them to seek out the simple remedies which are available for the terrible diseases by which foreigners are attacked and which are found growing under the same circumstances which produce the ills they minister to. So true is it that beside the nettle grows the cure for its sting.

I do not willingly care to dwell upon scenes of suffering and death, but it is with such scenes that my life's experience has made me most familiar and it is impossible to avoid their description now and then, and here I would fain record, in humble spirit, my conclusions, drawn from the bearing of those whom I have now and then accompanied a little distance on their way into the Valley of the Shadow of Death, on the awful and important question of religious feeling.

Death is always terrible, no one need be ashamed to fear it. How we bear it depends much upon our constitutions. I have seen some brave men, who have smiled at the cruellest amputation, die trembling like children, while others, whose lives have been spent in avoidance of the least danger or trouble, have drawn their last painful breath like heroes, striking at their foe to the last, robbing him of his victory and making their defeat a triumph. But I cannot trace all the peace and resignation which I have witnessed on many deathbeds to temperament alone, although I believe it has much more to do with them than many

teachers will allow. I have stood by receiving the last
blessings of Christians and closing the eyes of those who
had nothing to trust to but the mercy of a God who will be
far more merciful to us than we are to one another, and I say
decidedly that the Christian's death is the glorious one, as is
his life. You can never find a good man who is not a worker,
he is no laggard in the race of life. Three, two, or one score
years of life have been to him a season of labour in his
appointed sphere and as the work of the hands earns for us
sweet rest by night, so does the heart's labour of a lifetime
make the repose of heaven acceptable.

This is my experience. I remember the death of a man
whom I grew to love in a few short weeks, the thought of
which stirs my heart now and has sustained me in seasons
of great danger. For before that time, if I had never feared
death, I had not learnt to meet him with a brave, smiling
face and this he taught me.

I must not tell you his name, for his friends live yet and
have been kind to me in many ways. One of them we shall
meet on Crimean soil. He was a young surgeon and as busy,
light-hearted and joyous as a good man should be and when
he fell ill they brought him to my house, there I nursed him
and grew fond of him, almost as fond as the poor lady his
mother in England far away.

For some time we thought him safe, but at last the most
terrible symptoms of the cruel disease showed themselves
and he knew that he must die. His thoughts were never for
himself, but for those he had to leave behind, all his pity was
for them. It was trying to see his poor hands tremblingly
penning the last few words of leave-taking — trying to see
how piteously the poor worn heart longed to see once more
the old familiar faces of the loved ones in unconscious

happiness at home and yet I had to support him while this sad task was effected and to give him all the help I could. I think he had some fondness for me, or, perhaps, his kind heart feigned a feeling that he saw would give me joy, for I used to call him "My son — my dear child," and to weep over him in a very weak and silly manner.

He sent for an old friend, Captain S, and when he came, I had to listen to the dictation of his simple will — his dog to one friend, his ring to another, his books to a third, his love and kind wishes to all and, that over, my poor son prepared himself to die — a child in all save a man's calm courage. He beckoned me to raise him in the bed and, as I passed my arms around him, he saw the tears I could not repress, rolling down my brown cheeks and thanked me with a few words: "Let me lay my head upon your breast."

And so he rested, now then speaking lowly to himself, "It's only that I miss my mother, but Heaven's will be done."

He repeated this many times, until the Heaven he obeyed sent him in its mercy forgetfulness and his thoughts no longer wandered to his earthly home. I heard glad words feebly uttered and so in a little while my arms no longer held him.

I have a little gold brooch with his hair in it now. I wonder what inducement could be strong enough to cause me to part with that memorial, sent me by his mother some months later, with the following letter: —

MY DEAR MADAM,

Will you do me the favour to accept the enclosed trifle in remembrance of that dear son whose last moments were soothed by your kindness and as a mark of my gratitude.

Your ever sincere and obliged,

M — S

After this, I was sent for by the medical authorities to provide nurses for the sick at Up-Park Camp, about a mile from Kingston and, leaving some nurses and my sister at home, I went there and did my best, but it was little we could do to mitigate the severity of the epidemic.

About eight months after my return to Jamaica, it became necessary that someone should go to the Isthmus of Panama to wind up the affairs of my late hotel. Fearing another fit of restlessness, I prepared to return there myself.

I found Navy Bay but little altered. It was evening when I arrived there and my friend Mr. E., who came to meet me on the wharf, carefully piloted me through the wretched streets, giving me especial warning not to stumble over what looked like three long boxes, loosely covered with the debris of a fallen house. They had such a peculiar look about them that I stopped to ask what they were, receiving an answer which revived all my former memories of Darien life, "Oh, they're only three Irishmen killed in a row a week ago, whom its nobody's business to bury."

I went to Gorgona, wound up the affairs of the hotel and, before returning to Navy Bay, took the occasion of accompanying my brother to the town of Panama. We did not go with the crowd, but rode alone on mules, taking with us three native guides on foot.

Although the distance was not much over twenty miles and we started at daybreak, we did not reach Panama until nightfall. But far from being surprised at this, my chief wonder was that we ever succeeded in getting over the journey. Through sand and mud, over hill and plain, through thick forests, deep gulleys and over rapid streams, the road sometimes being made of logs of wood laid transversely, with faggots stuffed between, while here and there we had to work our way through a tangled network of brushwood and over broken rocks that seemed to have been piled together as stones for some giant's sling.

We found Panama an old fashioned, irregular town, with queer stone houses, almost all of which had been turned by the traders into stores.

On my return to Navy Bay — or Colon, as the New Granadans would have it called — I again opened a store and stayed there for three months or so. I did not find that society had improved much in my absence, indeed, it appeared to have grown more lawless. Endless quarrels, often resulting in bloodshed, took place between the strangers and the natives and disturbed the peace of the town. Once the Spanish were incensed to such an extent, that they planned a general rising against the foreigners and, but for the opportune arrival of an English war steamer, the consequences might have been terrible. The Americans were well-armed and ready, but the native population far outnumbered them.

Altogether, I was not sorry when an opportunity offered itself to do something at one of the stations of the New Granada Goldmining Company, Escribanos, about seventy miles from Navy Bay. I made the journey there in a little vessel, all communication by land from Navy Bay being impossible, on account of the thick, dense forests, that would have resisted the attempts of an army to cut its way through them.

As I was at this place for some months altogether and as it was the only portion of my life devoted to goldseeking, I shall make no apologies for endeavouring to describe the out of the way village life of New Granada.

Escribanos is in the province of Veraguas, in the State of New Granada — information uninteresting enough, I have little doubt, to all but a very few of my readers. It lies near the mouth of a rivulet bearing that name, which, leaving the river Belen, runs away to the sea on its own account, about a mile from the mouth of that river. It is a great neighbourhood for goldmines and about that time companies and private individuals were trying hard to turn them to good account. Near it is the Fort Bowen mine and several others, some yielding silver, others gold ore, in small quantities. Others lie in the vicinity of the Palmilla — another river, which discharges itself into the sea about ten miles from Escribanos and there were more eastward of it, near a similar river, the Coquelet. Legends were rife at that time and they may be revived at no distant date, of the treasures to be found at Cucuyo, Zapetero, Pananomé and many other Indian villages on their banks, which in times gone by had yielded up golden treasures to the Old World. But at this time the yield of gold did not repay the labour and capital necessary to extract it from tho quartz and it can only prove successful if more economical methods can be discovered than those now used for that purpose.

Carlos Alexander, the alcalde of Escribanos, had made a good thing out of the gold mania. The mine had belonged to him, had been sold at a fine price and, passing through several hands, had at last come into possession of the company who were now working it, its former owner settling down as ruler over the little community of two hundred souls that had collected at Escribanos. He was a black man, was fond of talking of his early life in slavery and how he had escaped, and possessed no ordinary intellect. He possessed, also, a house, which in England a well-bred hound would not have accepted as a kennel, a white wife and a pretty daughter, with a whitish-brown complexion and a pleasant name — Juliana.

Of this mine, Mr. Day — by whose invitation, when I saw him at Navy Bay, I went there — was at that time superintendent. He was a distant connection of my late husband and treated me with great kindness. Strangely enough, we met again in a far different part of the world and became more closely connected. But I am anticipating.

The major part of the population of Escribanos, including even the women and children, worked at the mine. The labour was hard and disagreeable. I often used to watch them at their work and would sometimes wander about by myself, thinking it possible that I might tumble across some gold in my rambles. And I once did come upon some heavy yellow material that brought my heart into my mouth with that strange thrilling delight which all who have hunted for the precious metal understand so well. I think it was very wrong, but I kept the secret of the place from the alcalde and everyone else and filled some bottles with the precious dust, to carry down to Navy Bay. I did not go for some time, but when I did, one of my first visits was to a gold buyer. You can imagine my feelings when he coolly laughed and told me it was some material (I forget its name) very like gold, but valueless. The worst part of it was that, in my annoyance and shame, I threw all I had away and among it some which I had reason to believe subsequently was genuine.

The landing at Escribanos was very difficult and when the surf ran high, impossible. I was once witness to a harrowing scene there. A little boat, manned by three sailors, grounded on a rock not far from shore during a terrible season, when to reach it from the land was, after many attempts, found impossible. The hapless crew lingered on for two days, suffering cruelly from hunger and thirst, their cries ringing in our ears above the storm's pitiless fury. On the third day, two of them took to the sea and were drowned, the third was not strong enough to leave the boat and died in it.

I did not stay long at Escribanos on my first visit as the alcalde's guest, but having made arrangements for a longer sojourn, I went back to Navy Bay, where I laid in a good stock of the stores I should have most use for and returned to Escribanos in safety. I stayed there some months, pleased with the novelty of the life and busy with schemes for seeking for, or — as the golddiggers call it, 'prospecting for' — other mines.

The foreigners were just as troublesome in this little out of the way place as they were and are, in every other part of Central America, and quarrels were as frequent in our little community as at Cruces or Navy Bay.

Indeed, Alexander had hard work to maintain peace in his small kingdom and, although ably seconded by Mr. Day, more than once American disregard of his sway was almost too strong for him. Very often the few foreigners would quarrel among themselves; and once they came to blows and an Irishman was stabbed by an American named Campfield, the alcalde roused himself to punish the culprit.

The native population were glad enough to have an American in their power and when I heard Alexander give his men instructions to shoot the culprit if he resisted, I started off to his hut and reached it in time to prevent bloodshed. He was taken and kept in confinement and soft-hearted Juliana and I had enough to do to prevent his being made a stern example of. But we got him off for a fine of five hundred dollars.

Again the little community of Escribanos was very near getting up a revolution against its constituted government — a very common amusement in Central America. Twelve sailors, deserters from an American ship, found their way there and, before long, plotted to dethrone Alexander and take possession of the mine. Mr. Day gained information of their plan. The whole population of Escribanos were roused and warned and, arming a score of the boldest natives, he surrounded the house in which they were and captured the conspirators, who were too much taken by surprise to offer resistance. He sent them down to Navy Bay, there to be handed over to the Government whose service they had left.

Of course, my medical skill did not rust for want of practice at Escribanos. The place was not healthy, and strangers to the climate suffered severely. A surgeon himself, sent there by the West Granada Goldmining Company, was glad to throw *his* physic to the dogs and be cured in my way by mine and I was fortunately able to nurse Mr. Day through a sharp attack of illness.

In consequence of the difficulty of communication with Navy Bay, our fare was of the simplest at Escribanos. It consisted mainly of salt meat, rice and roasted Indian corn. The native fare was not tempting and some of their delicacies were absolutely disgusting. With what pleasure, for instance, could one foreign to their tastes and habits dine off a roasted monkey, whose grilled head bore a strong resemblance to a negro baby's? And yet the Indians used to bring them to us for sale, strung on a stick. They were worse still stewed in soup, when it was positively frightful to dip your ladle in unsuspectingly and bring up what closely resembled a brown baby's limb. I got on better with the parrots and could agree with the "Senorita, buono buono" with which the natives recommended them and yet their flesh, what little there was of it, was very coarse and hard. Nor did I always refuse to concede praise to a squirrel, if well cooked. But although the flesh of the iguana — another favourite dish — was white and tender as a chicken, I never could stomach it. These iguanas are immense green lizards, or rather moderate-sized crocodiles sometimes three feet in length, but weighing generally about seven or eight pounds. The Indians used to bring them down in boats, alive, on their backs, with their legs tied behind them, so that they had the most comical look of distress it is possible to imagine. The Spanish Indians have a proverb referring to an iguana so bound, the purport of which has slipped from my memory, but which shows the habit to be an old one. Their eggs are highly prized and their captors have a cruel habit of extracting these delicacies from them while alive and roughly sewing up the wound, which I never could muster sufficient courage to witness.

The rivers near Escribanos were well-stocked with crocodiles, the sea had its fair share of sharks, while on land you too often met with snakes and other venomous reptiles. The sting of some of them was very dangerous. One man, who was bitten when I was there, swelled to an enormous size and bled even at the roots of his hair. The remedy of the natives appeared to be copious bleeding.

Before I left Escribanos I made a journey, in company with a gentleman named Little, my maid and the alcalde's daughter, into the interior of the country, for a short distance, following the course of the Palmilla river. This was for the purpose of prospecting a mine on that river, said to be obtainable at an easy price. Its course was a very winding one and we often had to leave the canoe and walk through the shallow waters, that every now and then interfered with our progress. As we progressed, Little carefully sounded the channel of the river, with the view of ascertaining to what extent it was navigable.

The tropical scenery was very grand, but I am afraid I only marked what was most curious in it — at least, that is foremost in my memory now. I know I wondered much what motive Nature could have had in twisting the roots and branches of the trees into such strange fantastic contortions. I watched with unfailing interest the birds and animals we disturbed in our progress, from the huge wild boar that went tearing through the brushwood, to the tiniest bright-hued bird that dashed like a flash of many-coloured fire before our eyes. And very much surprised was I when the Indians stopped before a large tree and, on their making an incision in the bark with a matcheto (hatchet), there exuded a thick creamy liquid, which they wished me to taste, saying that this was the famous milk-tree. I needed some persuasion at first, but when I had tasted some upon a biscuit, I was so charmed with its flavour that I should soon have taken more than was good for me had not Mr. Little interfered with some judicious advice.

We reached the mine and brought back specimens of the quartz, some of which I have now.

Soon after this I left Escribanos and, stopping but a short time at Navy Bay, came on direct to England. I had claims on a Mining Company which are still unsatisfied, I had to look after my share in the Palmilla Mine speculation and, above all, I had long been troubled with a secret desire to embark in a very novel speculation, about which I have as yet said nothing to the reader.

Before I finally leave the republic of New Granada, I may be allowed to write a few words on the present aspect of affairs on the Isthmus of Panama.

Recent news from America bring the intelligence that the Government of the United States has at length succeeded in finding a reasonable excuse for exercising a protectorate over, or in other words annexing, the Isthmus of Panama.

To anyone at all acquainted with American policy in Central America, this intelligence can give no surprise, our only wonder being that some such excuse was not made years ago. At this crisis, then, a few remarks from the humblest observer of life in the republic of New Granada must possess some interest for the curious, if not value.

I found something to admire in the people of Granada, but not much, and I found very much more to condemn most unequivocally. Whatever was of any worth in their institutions, such as the comparative freedom, religious toleration, etc., was owing mainly to the negroes who had sought the protection of the republic. I found the Spanish Indians treacherous, passionate and indolent, with no higher aim or object but simply to enjoy the present after their own torpid, useless fashion. Like most fallen nations, they are very conservative in their habits and principles, while the blacks are enterprising and in their opinions incline not unnaturally to democracy. But for their old antipathy, there is no doubt that the negroes would lean towards America, but they gladly encourage the prejudice of the New Granadans and foster it in every way. Hence the ceaseless quarrels which have disturbed Chagres and Panama, until it has become necessary for an American force to garrison those towns. For humanity and civilization's sake, there can be little doubt as to the expediency of this step, but I should not be at all surprised to hear that the republic was preparing to make some show of resistance against its powerful brother, for, as the reader will have perceived the New Granadans' experiences of American manners have not been favourable and they do not know, as we do, how little real sympathy the Government of the United States has with the extreme class of its citizens who have made themselves so conspicuous in the great highroad to California.

CHAPTER 8

Before I left Jamaica for Navy Bay, as narrated in the last chapter, war had been declared against Russia and we were all anxiously expecting news of a descent upon the Crimea. Now, no sooner had I heard of war somewhere, than I longed to witness it. When I was told that many of the regiments I had known so well in Jamaica had left England for the scene of action, the desire to join them became stronger than ever. I used to stand for hours in silent thought before an old map of the world, in a little corner of which someone had chalked a red cross, to enable me to distinguish where the Crimea was and as I traced the route thither, all difficulties would vanish. But when I came to talk over the project with my friends, the best scheme I could devise seemed so wild and improbable that I was fain to resign my hopes for a time, and so started for Navy Bay.

But all the way to England, from Navy Bay, I was turning my old wish over and over in my mind. When I found myself in London, in the autumn of 1854, just after the baffle of Alma had been fought and my old friends were fairly before the walls of Sebastopol, how to join them there took up far more of my thoughts than that visionary goldmining speculation on the river Palmilla, which seemed so feasible to us in New Granada, but was considered so wild and unprofitable a speculation in London.

As time wore on, the inclination to join my old friends of

the 97th, 48th and other regiments, battling with worse foes than yellow fever or cholera, took such exclusive possession of my mind, that I threw over the gold speculation altogether and devoted all my energies to my new scheme.

Heaven knows it was visionary enough! I had no friends who could help me in such a project, nay, who would understand why I desired to go and what I desired to do when I got there. My funds, although they might, carefully husbanded, carry me over the three thousand miles and land me at Balaclava, would not support me there long, while to persuade the public that an unknown Creole woman would be useful to their army before the walls of Sebastopol, was too improbable an achievement to be thought of for an instant. Circumstances, however, assisted me.

As the winter wore on, came hints from various quarters of mismanagement, want and suffering in the Crimea. After the battles of Balaclava and Inkermann and the fearful storm of the 14th of November, the worst anticipations were realized. We knew that the hospitals were full to suffocation, that scarcity and exposure were the fate of all in the camp and that the brave fellows for whom any of us at home would have split our last shilling and shared our last meal, were dying thousands of miles away from the active sympathy of their fellow countrymen.

Fast and thick upon the news of Inkermann, fought by a handful of fasting and enfeebled men against eight times their number of picked Russians, brought fresh and animated to the contest, and while all England was reeling beneath the shock of that fearful victory, came the sad news that hundreds were dying whom the Russian shot and sword had spared, and that the hospitals of Scutari were utterly unable to shelter, or their inadequate staff to attend to, the shiploads of sick and wounded which were sent to them across the stormy Black Sea.

Directly England knew the worst, she set about repairing her past neglect. In every household, busy fingers were working for the poor soldier — money flowed in golden streams wherever need was — and Christian ladies, mindful of the sublime example, *I was sick and ye visited me*, hastened to volunteer their services by those sickbeds which only women know how to soothe and bless.

Need I be ashamed to confess that I shared in the general enthusiasm and longed more than ever to carry my busy (and the reader will not hesitate to add experienced) fingers where the sword or bullet had been busiest and pestilence most rife. I had seen much of sorrow and death elsewhere, but they had never daunted me and if I could feel happy binding up the wounds of quarrelsome Americans and treacherous Spaniards, what delight should I not experience if I could be useful to my own 'sons', suffering for a cause it was so glorious to fight and bleed for!

I never stayed to discuss probabilities, or enter into conjectures as to my chances of reaching the scene of action. I made up my mind that if the army wanted nurses, they would be glad of me. With all the ardour of my nature, which ever carried me where inclination prompted, I decided that I would go to the Crimea and go I did, as all the world knows.

Of course, had it not been for my old strong-mindedness (which has nothing to do with obstinacy and is in no way related to it, the best term I can think of to express it being 'judicious decisiveness'), I should have given up the scheme a score of times in as many days, so regularly did each successive day give birth to a fresh set of rebuffs and disappointments. I shall make no excuse to my readers for giving them a pretty full history of my struggles to become a Crimean heroine!

My first idea (and knowing that I was well fitted for the work and would be the right woman in the right place, the reader can fancy my audacity) was to apply to the War Office for the post of hospital nurse. Among the diseases which I understood were most prevalent in the Crimea were cholera, diarrhoea and dysentery, all of them more or less known in tropical climates and with which, as the reader will remember, my Panama experience had made me tolerably familiar. Now, no one will accuse me of presumption, if I say that I thought (and so it afterwards proved) that my knowledge of these human ills would not only render my services as a nurse more valuable, but would enable me to be of use to the overworked doctors. The others thought so too, I took with me ample testimony. I cannot resist the temptation of giving my readers one of the testimonials I had, it seems so eminently practical and to the point:

I became acquainted with Mrs. Seacole through the instrumentality of T. B. Cowan, Esq., E. B. M. Consul at Colon, on the Isthmus of Panama and have had many opportunities of witnessing her professional zeal and ability in the treatment of aggravated forms of tropical diseases.

I am myself personally much indebted for her indefatigable kindness and skill at a time when I am apt to believe the advice of a practitioner qualified in the North would have little availed.

Her peculiar fitness, in a constitutional point of view, for the duties of a medical attendant, needs no comment.

A. G. M.,
Late Medical Officer, West Granada
Goldmining Company.

So I made long and unwearied application at the War Office, in blissful ignorance of the labour and time I was throwing away. I have reason to believe that I considerably interfered with the repose of sundry messengers and disturbed to an alarming degree the official gravity of some nice gentlemanly young fellows, who were working out their salaries in an easy, off-hand way. My ridiculous endeavours to gain an interview with the Secretary at War of course failed and glad at last to oblige a distracted messenger, I transferred my attentions to the Quartermaster General's department. Here I saw another gentleman, who listened to me with a great deal of polite enjoyment and — his amusement ended — hinted, had I not better apply to the Medical Department and, accordingly, I attached myself to their quarters with the same unwearying ardour. But, of course, I grew tired at last and then I changed my plans.

Now, I am not for a single instant going to blame the authorities who would not listen to the offer of a motherly yellow woman to go to the Crimea and nurse her 'sons' there, suffering from cholera, diarrhoea and a host of lesser ills. In my country, where people know our use, it would have been different, but here it was natural enough — although I had references and other voices spoke for me — that they should laugh, good-naturedly enough, at my offer. War, I know, is a serious game, but sometimes very humble actors are of great use in it and if the reader, when he comes in time to peruse the evidence of those who had to do with the Sebastopol drama, of my share in it, will turn back to this chapter, he will confess perhaps that, after all, the impulse which led me to the War Department was not unnatural.

My new scheme was, I candidly confess, worse devised than the one which had failed. Miss Nightingale had left England for the Crimea, but other nurses were still to follow and my new plan was simply to offer myself to Mrs. H. as a recruit. Feeling that I was one of the very women they most wanted, experienced and fond of the work, I jumped at once to the conclusion that they would gladly enroll me in their number. To go to Cox's, the army agents, who were most obliging to me and obtain the Secretary at War's private address, did not take long and, that done, I laid the same pertinacious siege to his great house as I had previously done to his place of business.

Many a long hour did I wait in his great hall, while scores passed in and out, many of them looking curiously at me. The flunkeys (noble creatures!) marvelled exceedingly at the yellow woman whom no excuses could get rid of, nor impertinence dismay, showing me very clearly that they resented my persisting in remaining there in mute appeal from their sovereign will.

At last I gave that up, after a message from Mrs. H. that the full complement of nurses had been secured and that my offer could not be entertained. Once again I tried and had an interview, this time with one of Miss Nightingale's companions. She gave me the same reply and I read in her face the fact that, had there been a vacancy, I should not have been chosen to fill it.

As a last resort, I applied to the managers of the Crimean Fund to know whether they would give me a passage to the camp — once there I would trust to something turning up. But this failed also and, one cold evening, I stood in the twilight, which was fast deepening into wintry night and looked back upon the ruins of my lost castle in the sir. The disappointment seemed a cruel one. I was so conscious of the unselfishness of the motives which induced me to leave England — so certain of the service I could render along the sick soldiery and yet I found it so difficult to convince others of these facts.

Doubts and suspicions arose in my heart for the first and last time, thank heaven. Was it possible that American prejudices against colour had some root here? Did these ladies shrink from accepting my aid because my blood flowed beneath a somewhat duskier skin than theirs? Tears streamed down my foolish cheeks, as I stood in the fast emptying streets, tears of grief that any should doubt my motives — that Heaven should deny me the opportunity that I sought. Then I stood still and, looking upward through and through the dark clouds that shadowed London, prayed aloud for help. I dare say that I was a strange sight to the few passers-by, who hastened homeward through the gloom and mist of that wintry night. I dare say those who read these pages will wonder at me as much as they who saw me did, but you must all remember that I am one of an impulsive people and find it hard to put that restraint upon my feelings which to you is so easy and natural.

The morrow, however, brought fresh hope. A good night's rest had served to strengthen my determination. Let what might happen, to the Crimea I would go. If in no other way, then would I upon my own responsibility and at my own cost. There were those there who had known me in Jamaica, who had been under my care, doctors who would vouch for my skill and willingness to aid them and a general who had more than once helped me and would do so still. Why not trust to their welcome and kindness and start at once? If the authorities had allowed me, I would willingly have given them my services as a nurse, but as they declined them, should I not open a hotel for invalids in the Crimea in my own way?

I had no more idea of what the Crimea was than the home authorities themselves perhaps, but having once made up my mind, it was not long before cards were printed and speeding across the Mediterranean to my friends before Sebastopol. Here is one of them:

> *BRITISH HOTEL.*
> *MRS. MARY SEACOLE*
> *(Late of Kingston. Jamaica)*
> *Respectfully announces to her former kind*
> *friends and to the officers of the Army and*
> *Navy generally, that she has taken her*
> *passage in the steamer Hollander, to start*
> *from London on the 25th of January,*
> *intending on her arrival at Balaclava to*
> *establish a mess table and comfortable*
> *quarters for sick and convalescent officers.*

This bold programme would reach the Crimea in the end of January, at a time when any officer would have considered a stall in an English stable luxurious quarters compared to those he possessed, and had nearly forgotten the comforts of a mess table. It must have read to them rather like a mockery and yet, as the reader will see, I succeeded in redeeming my pledge.

While this new scheme was maturing, I again met Mr.

Day in England. He was bound to Balaclava upon some shipping business and we came to the understanding that (if it were found desirable) we should together open a store as well as a hotel in the neighbourhood of the camp. So was originated the well-known firm of Seacole and Day which, for so many months, did business upon the now deserted highroad from the then busy harbour of Balaclava to the front of the British army before Sebastopol.

These new arrangements were not allowed to interfere in any way with the main object of my journey. A great portion of my limited capital was, with the kind aid of a medical friend, invested in medicines which I had reason to believe would be useful, with the remainder I purchased those home comforts which I thought would be most difficult to obtain away from England.

I had scarcely set my foot on board the *Hollander* before I met a friend. The supercargo was the brother of the Mr. S, whose death in Jamaica the reader will not have forgotten, and he gave me a hearty welcome. I thought the meeting augured well and when I told him my plans he gave me the most cheering encouragement. I was glad, indeed, of any support for, beyond all doubt, my project was a hazardous one.

So cheered at the outset, I watched without a pang the shores of England sink behind the smooth sea and turned my gaze hopefully to the, as yet landless horizon, beyond which lay that little peninsula to which the eyes and hearts of all England were so earnestly directed.

So, cheerily! the good ship ploughed its way eastward ho! for Turkey.

CHAPTER 9

I am not going to risk the danger of wearying the reader
with a long account of the voyage to Constantinople,
already worn threadbare by bookmaking tourists. It was a
very interesting one and, as I am a good sailor, I had not
even the temporary horrors of sea-sickness to mar it. The
weather, although cold, was fine and the sea good-
humouredly calm and I enjoyed the voyage amazingly. As
day by day we drew nearer to the scene of action, my doubts
of success grew less and less, until I had a conviction of the
rightness of the step I had taken, which would have carried
me buoyantly through any difficulties.

On the way, of course, I was called up from my berth at
an unreasonable hour to gaze upon the Cape of St. Vincent
and expected to feel duly impressed when the long bay
where Trafalgar's fight was won came in view, with the
white convent walls on the cliffs above bathed in the early
sunlight. I never failed to take an almost childish interest in
the signals which passed between the *Hollander* and the fleet
of vessels whose sails whitened the track to and from the
Crimea, trying to puzzle out the language these children of
the ocean spoke in their hurried course and wondering
whether any, or what sufficiently important thing could
happen which would warrant their stopping on their busy
way.

We spent a short time at Gibraltar and you may imagine

that I was soon on shore making the best use of the few hours reprieve granted to the *Hollander's* weary engines. I had an idea that I should do better alone, so I declined all offers of companionship and, selecting a brisk young fellow from the mob of cicerones who offered their services, saw more of the art of fortification in an hour or so than I could understand in as many years. The pleasure was rather fatiguing and I was not sorry to return to the marketplace, where I stood curiously watching its strange and motley population. While so engaged, I heard for the first time an exclamation which became familiar enough to me afterwards.

"Why, bless my soul, old fellow, if this is not our good old Mother Seacole!"

I turned round and saw two officers whose features set in a broad frame of Crimean beard, I had some difficulty in recognising. But I soon remembered that they were two of the 48th, who had been often in my house at Kingston. Glad were the kind-hearted fellows and not a little surprised withal, to meet their old hostess in the marketplace of Gibraltar, bound for the scene of action which they had left invalided. It was not long before we were talking old times over some wine — Spanish, I suppose — but it was very nasty.

"And you are going to the front, old lady? You, of all people in the world."

"Why not, my sons? Won't they be glad to have me there?"

"By Jove, yes, mother," answered one, an Irishman. "It isn't many women — God bless them! — we've had to spoil us out there. But it's not the place even for you, who know what hardship is? You'll never get a roof to cover you at

Balaclava, nor on the road either."

So they rattled on, telling me of the difficulties that were in store for me. But they could not shake my resolution.

"Do you think I shall be of any use to you when I get there?"

"Surely."

"Then I'll go, were the place a hundred times worse than you describe it. Can't I rig up a hut with the packing case and sleep, if need be, on straw, like Margery Daw?"

They laughed and drank success to me and to our next meeting. For, although they were going home invalided, the brave fellows' hearts were with their companions, despite all the hardships they had passed through.

We stopped at Malta also, where of course I landed and stared about me and submitted to be robbed by the lazy Maltese with all a traveller's resignation. Here, also, I met friends — some medical officers who had known me in Kingston and one of them, Dr. B, lately arrived from Scutari, gave me, when he heard my plans, a letter of introduction to Miss Nightingale, then hard at work, evoking order out of confusion and bravely resisting the despotism of death, at the hospital of Scutari.

So on, past beautiful islands and shores, until we are steaming against a swift current and an adverse wind, between two tower-crested promontories of rock, which they tell me stand in Europe and in Asia and are connected with some pretty tale of love in days long gone by. Travel where a woman may, in the New World, or the Old, she meets this old, old tale everywhere. It is the one bond of sympathy which I have found existing in three quarters of the world alike. So on, until the cable rattles over the windlass, as the good ship's anchor plunges down fathoms deep into the blue waters of the Bosphorus — her voyage ended.

I do not think that Constantinople impressed me so much as I had expected. I thought its streets would match those of Navy Bay not unfairly. The caicques, also, of which I had ample experience — for I spent six days here, wandering about Pera and Stamboul in the daytime and returning to the *Hollander* at nightfall — might be made more safe and commodious for stout ladies, even if the process interfered a little with their ornament.

Time and trouble combined have left me with a well filled out, portly form — the envy of many an angular Yankee female — and, more than once, it was in no slight danger of becoming too intimately acquainted with the temperature of the Bosphorus. But I will do the Turkish boatmen the justice to say that they were as politely careful of my safety as their astonishment and regard for the well-being of their caicques (which they appear to love as an Arab does his horse, or an Eskimo his dogs and for the same reason perhaps) would admit. Somewhat surprised, also, seemed the cunning-eyed Greeks, who throng the streets of Pera, at the unprotected Creole woman who took Constantinople so coolly (it would require something more to surprise her), while the grave English raised their eyebrows wonderingly and the more vivacious French shrugged their pliant shoulders into the strangest contortions. I accepted it all as a compliment to a stout female tourist, neatly dressed in a red or yellow dress, a plain shawl of some other colour and a simple straw wide awake, with bright red streamers. I flatter myself that I woke up sundry sleepy-eyed Turks, who seemed to think that the great object of life was to avoid showing surprise at anything, while the Turkish women gathered around me and jabbered about me, in the most flattering manner.

How I ever succeeded in getting Mr. Day's letters from the post office in Constantinople, puzzles me now, but I did. I shall ever regard my success as one of the great triumphs of my life. Their contents were not very cheering. He gave a very dreary account of Balaclava and of camp life and almost dissuaded me from continuing my journey, but his last letter ended by giving me instructions as to the purchases I had best make, if I still determined upon making the adventure, so I forgot all the rest and busied myself in buying in the stores he recommended.

I found time, before I left the *Hollander*, to charter a crazy caicque, to carry me to Scutari, intending to present Dr. F's letter to Miss Nightingale.

It was afternoon when the boatmen set me down in safety at the landing place of Scutari and I walked up the slight ascent to the great dull-looking hospital. Thinking of the many noble fellows who had been borne, or had painfully crept along this path, only to die within that dreary building, I felt rather dull and directly I entered the hospital and came upon the long wards of sufferers, lying there so quiet and still, a rush of tears came to my eyes and blotted out the sight for a few minutes. But I soon felt at home and looked about me with great interest. The men were, many of them, very quiet. Some of the convalescent formed themselves into little groups around one who read a newspaper, others had books in their hands, or by their side, where they had fallen when slumber overtook the readers, while hospital orderlies moved to and fro and now and then the female nurses, in their quiet uniform, passed noiselessly on some mission of kindness.

I was fortunate enough to find an old acquaintance, who accompanied me through the wards and rendered it unnecessary for me to trouble the busy nurses. This was an old 97th man — a Sergeant T, whom I had known in Kingston and who was slowly recovering from an attack of dysentery and making himself of use here until the doctors should let him go back and "have another go at the Russians." He was very glad to meet me and told me his history very socially and took me to the bedsides of some comrades, who had also known me at Up-Park Camp.

My poor fellows, how their eyes glisten when they light upon an old friend's face in these Turkish barracks put to so sad a use, three thousand miles from home.

One of them ("hurt in the trenches," the Sergeant said), with a shaven, bandaged head and bright, restless Irish eyes, hollers out, "Mother Seacole! Mother Seacole!" in such an excited tone of voice and when he has shaken hands a score of times, falls back upon his pillow very wearily. I sit by his side and try to cheer him with talk about the future, when he shall grow well and see home and hear them all thank him for what he has been helping to do, so that he grows all right in a few minutes. But, hearing that I am on the way to the front, gets excited again. You see, illness and weakness make these strong men as children, not least in the patient unmurmuring resignation with which they suffer. I think my Irish friend had a indistinct idea of a muddle somewhere, which had kept him for weeks on salt meat and biscuit, until it gave him the scurvy, for he is very anxious that I should take over plenty of vegetables, of every sort.

It is strange to hear his almost plaintive tone as he urges: "Bring plenty of eggs, we never saw eggs over there."

At some slight risk of giving offence, I cannot resist the

temptation of lending a helping hand here and there —
replacing a slipped bandage, or using a stiff one. But I do not
think anyone was offended and one doctor, who had with
some surprise and, at first, alarm on his face, watched me
replace a bandage, which was giving pain, said, very kindly,
when I had finished, "Thank you, ma'am."

One thought never left my mind as I walked through the
fearful miles of suffering in that great hospital. If it is so
here, what must it not be at the scene of war — on the spot
where the poor fellows are stricken down by pestilence or
Russian bullets and days and nights of agony must be
passed before a woman's hand can dress their wounds. I felt
happy in the conviction that I would be useful three or four
days nearer to their pressing wants than this.

It was growing late. Dr. S, who had kindly borne me
company for the last half hour, agreed with me that the
caicque was not the safest conveyance by night on the
Bosphorus and recommended me to present my letter to
Miss Nightingale and perhaps a lodging for the night could
be found for me. So, still under the Sergeant's patient
guidance, we threaded our way through passages and
corridors, all used as sick wards, until we reached the corner
tower of the building, in which are the nurses' quarters.

I think Mrs. B, who saw me, felt more surprise than she
could politely show (I never found women so quick to
understand me as the men) when I handed her Dr. F's kind
letter respecting me, and apologized for troubling Miss
Nightingale. There is that in the Doctor's letter (he had been
much at Scutari) which prevents my request being refused
and I was asked to wait until Miss Nightingale, whose every
moment is valuable, can see me. Meanwhile Mrs. B.
questioned me very kindly, but with the same look of

curiosity and surprise.

What object has Mrs. Seacole in coming out? This is the purport of her questions. Frankly, to be of use somewhere, I replied, for other considerations I had not, until necessity forced them upon me. Willingly, had they accepted me, I would have worked for the wounded in return for bread and water. I fancy Mrs. B. thought that I sought for employment at Scutari, for she said, very kindly:

"Miss Nightingale has the entire management of our hospital staff, but I do not think that any vacancy. . ."

"Excuse me, ma'am," I interrupt her, "but I am bound for the front in a few days. . ."

My questioner departed, more surprised than ever.

The room I waited in was used as a kitchen. Upon the stoves were cans of soup, broth and arrowroot, while nurses passed in and out in a noiseless, sad and subdued manner. I thought many of them had that strange expression of the eyes which those who have gazed long on scenes of woe or horror seldom lose.

Within half an hour I was admitted to Miss Nightingale's presence. A slight figure in the nurses' dress, with a pale, gentle and firm face, resting lightly in the palm of one white hand, while the other supported the elbow — a position which gives to her countenance a keen inquiring expression, which is rather marked. Standing thus in repose and yet keenly observant — the greatest sign of impatience at any time, a slight, perhaps unwitting motion of the firmly planted right foot — was Florence Nightingale. That Englishwoman whose name shall never die, but sounds like music on the lips of British men until the hour of doom.

She reads Dr. F's letter and asks, in her gentle but eminently practical and business-like way:

"What do you want, Mrs. Seacole — anything that we can do for you? If it lies in my power, I shall be very happy."

So I tell her of my dread of the night journey and the improbability of my finding the *Hollander* in the dark and, with some diffidence, threw myself upon the hospitality of Scutari, offering to nurse the sick for the night. For many reasons, room even for one in the hospital was at that time no easy matter to find, but at last a bed was found to be unoccupied in the washerwomen's quarters.

My experience of washerwomen, all the world over, is the same — that they are kind, soft-hearted folks. Possibly the soapsuds they almost live in find their way into their hearts and tempers and soften them. This Scutari washerwoman is no exception to the rule and welcomes me most heartily. With her, also, are some invalid nurses and after they have gone to bed, we spend some hours of the night talking over our adventures and giving one another scraps of our respective biographies. I hadn't long retired to my couch before I wished most heartily that we had continued our chat, for unbidden and most unwelcome companions took the washerwoman's place and persisted not only in dividing my bed, but my plump person also. Upon my word, I believe the fleas are the only industrious creatures in all Turkey. Some of their relatives would seem to have migrated into Russia, for I found them in the Crimea equally prosperous and ubiquitous. In the morning, a breakfast is sent to my mangled remains and a kind message from Mrs. B, having reference to how I spent the night. After an interview with some other medical men, whose acquaintance I had made in Jamaica, I shake hands with the soft-hearted washerwoman, up to her shoulders in soapsuds already, and start for the *Hollander*.

CHAPTER 10

During my stay in Constantinople, I was accustomed to employ, as a guide, a young Greek Jew, whose name it is no use my attempting to spell, but whom I called by the one common name there — 'Johnny'. Wishing, however, to distinguish my Johnny from the legion of other Johnnies, I preferred the term Jew to his other name and addressed him as Jew Johnny. How he had picked up his knowledge I cannot tell, but he could talk a little broken English, besides French, which, had I been qualified to criticise it, I should have found, perhaps, as broken as his English. He attached himself very closely to me and seemed very anxious to share my fortunes and after he had pleaded hard, many times, to be taken to the Crimea, I gave in and formally hired him. He was the best and most faithfull servant I had in the Crimea and, so far from regretting having picked up Jew Johnny from the streets of Pera, I should have been very badly off without him.

More letters come from Mr. Day, giving even worse accounts of the state of things at Balaclava, but it is too late for hesitation now. My plans are perfected, my purchases made and passage secured in the *Albatross* — a transport laden with cattle and commissariat officers for Balaclava. I thought I should never have transported my things from the *Hollander* to the *Albatross*. It was a terrible day and against the strong current and hurricane of wind Turkish and Greek arms seemed of little avail, but at last, after an hour or more of terrible anxiety and fear, the *Albatross's* side was reached, and I clambered on deck, drenched and wretched.

My companions are cheerful, pleasant fellows and the short, although somewhat hazardous, voyage across the Black Sea is safely made and one morning we become excited at seeing a dark rockbound coast, on which they tell us is Balaclava. As we steam on we see, away to the right, clouds of light smoke, which the knowing travellers tell us are not altogether natural, but show that Sebastopol is not yet taken, until the *Albatross* lay to within sight of where the *Prince*, with her ill-fated companions went down in that fearful November storm, four short months ago, while application is made to the harbourmaster for leave to enter the port of Balaclava. It does not appear the simplest favour in the world that we are applying for — licence to escape from the hazards of the Black Sea. But at last it comes and we slowly wind through a narrow channel and emerge into a small land-locked basin, so filled with shipping that their masts bend in the breeze like a wintry forest. Whatever might have been the case at one time, there is order in Balaclava Harbour now and the *Albatross,* with the aid of her boats, moves along to her appointed moorings.

Such a busy scene as that small harbour presented could be rarely met with elsewhere. Crowded with shipping, of every size and variety, from the noble English steamer to the smallest longshore craft, while between them and the shore passed and repassed innumerable boats, trim and stern men-o'-war's, merchant ship's laden to the gunwales, Greek and Maltese boats carrying their owners everywhere on their missions of sharp dealing and roguery. Coming from the quiet gloomy sea into this little nook of life and bustle, the transition is very sudden and startling and gives one enough to think about without desiring to go on shore this afternoon.

On the following morning, Mr. Day, apprised of my arrival, came on board the *Albatross* and our plans were laid.

I must leave the *Albatross*, of course, and until we decide upon our future, I had better take up my quarters onboard the *Medora*, which is hired by Government, at a great cost, as an ammunition ship. The proposal was not a very agreeable one, but I have no choice left me. Our stores, too, had to be landed at once. Warehouses were unheard of in Balaclava and we had to stack them upon the shore and protect them as well as we were able.

My first task, directly I had become settled on board the *Medora*, was to send word to my friends of my arrival in the Crimea and solicit their aid. I gave a Greek idler one pound to carry a letter to the camp of the 97th, while I sent another to Captain Peel, who was hard at work battering the defences of Sebastopol about the ears of the Russians, from the batteries of the Royal Naval Brigade. I addressed others to many of the medical men who had known me in other lands, nor did I neglect to send word to my kind patron, Sir John Campbell, then commanding a division.

My old friends answered my letters most kindly. As the various officers came down on duty or business to Balaclava they did not fail to find me out and welcome me to the Crimea, while Captain Peel and Sir J. Campbell sent the kindest messages and when they saw me, promised me every assistance, the General adding that he is glad to see me where there is so much to do. Among others, poor Mr. Vicars, whose kind face had so often lighted up my old house in Kingston, came to take me by the hand in this out

of the way corner of the world. I never felt so sure of the
success of any step as I did of this, before I had been a week
in Balaclava. But I had plenty of difficulties to contend with
on every side.

Among the first, one of the ships, in which were many of
our stores, the *Nonpareil*, was ordered out of the harbour
before we could land them all and there was more than a
probability that she would carry back to Constantinople
many of the things we had most pressing occasion for. It
became necessary, therefore, that someone should see
Admiral Boxer and try to interest that mild-spoken and
affable officer in our favour.

When I mentioned it to Mr. Day, he did not seem inclined
to undertake the mission and nothing was left but for me to
face the terrible Port-Admiral. Fortunately, Captain H, of the
Diamond, was inclined to be my friend and, not a little
amused with his mission, carried me right off to the
Admiral. I confess that I was as nearly frightened out of my
wits as I ever have been, for the Admiral's kind heart beat
under a decidedly rough husk and when Captain H told
him that I wanted his permission for the *Nonpareil* to remain
in the harbour for a few days, as there were stores on board,
he let fly enough hard words to frighten any woman. But
when I spoke up and told him that I had known his son in
the West Indies, he relented and granted my petition. But it
was not without more hard words and much grumbling that
a parcel of women should be coming out to a place where
they were not wanted.

Now, the Admiral did not repeat this remark a few days
afterwards, when he saw me attending the sick and
wounded upon the sick wharf.

I remained six weeks in Balaclava, spending my days on

shore and my nights on board ship. Over our stores stacked on the shore, a few sheets of rough tarpaulin were suspended and beneath these — my sole protection against the Crimean rain and wind — I spent some portion of each day, receiving visitors and selling stores.

But my chief occupation and one with which I never allowed any business to interfere, was helping the doctors to transfer the sick and wounded from the mules and ambulances into the transports that had to carry them to the hospitals of Scutari and Buyukdere. I did not forget the main object of my journey, to which I would have devoted myself exclusively had I been allowed, and very familiar did I become before long with the sick wharf of Balaclava.

My acquaintance with it began very shortly after I had reached Balaclava. The very first day that I approached the wharf, a party of sick and wounded had just arrived. Here was work for me, I felt sure. With so many patients, the doctors must be glad of all the hands they could get. Indeed, so strong was the old impulse within me, that I waited for no permission, but seeing a poor artilleryman stretched upon a pallet, groaning heavily, I ran up to him at once and eased the stiff dressing. Lightly my practiced fingers ran over the familiar work and well was I rewarded when the poor fellow's groans subsided into a restless uneasy mutter.

God help him! He had been hit in the forehead and I think his sight was gone. I stooped down and raised some tea to his baked lips (here and there upon the wharf were rows of little pannikins containing this beverage). Then his hand touched mine and rested there and I heard him mutter indistinctly, as though the discovery had arrested his wandering senses:

"Ha, this is surely a woman's hand."

I couldn't say much, but I tried to whisper something about hope and trust in God, but all the while I think his thoughts were running on this strange discovery. Perhaps I had brought to his poor mind memories of his home and the loved ones there, who would ask no greater favour than the privilege of helping him thus, for he continued to hold my hand in his feeble grasp and whisper "God bless you, woman, whoever you are. God bless you," over and over again.

I do not think that the surgeons noticed me at first although, as this was my introduction to Balaclava, I had not neglected my personal appearance and wore my favourite yellow dress and blue bonnet with the red ribbons, but I noticed one coming to me who, I think, would have laughed very merrily had it not been for the poor fellow at my feet. As it was, he came forward and shook hands very kindly, saying, "How do you do, ma'am? Much obliged to you for looking after my poor fellow, very glad to see you here."

And glad they always were, the kind-hearted doctors, to let me help them look after the sick and wounded sufferers brought to that fearful wharf.

I wonder if I can ever forget the scenes I witnessed there? Oh, they were heart-rending. I declare that I saw rough bearded men stand by and cry like the softest-hearted women at the sights of suffering they saw, while some who scorned comfort for themselves, would fidget about for hours before the long trains of mules and ambulances came in, nervous lest the most trifling thing that could minister to the sufferers' comfort should be neglected.

I have often heard men talk and preach very learnedly and conclusively about the great wickedness and selfishness of the human heart, I used to wonder whether they would have modified those opinions if they had been my companions for one day of the six weeks I spent upon that wharf and seen but one day's experience of the Christian sympathy and brotherly love shown by the strong to the weak. The task was a trying one and familiarity, you might think, would have worn down their keener feelings of pity and sympathy, but it was not so.

I was in the midst of my sad work one day when the Admiral came up and stood looking on. He vouchsafed no word nor look of recognition in answer to my salute, but stood silent by his hands behind his back, watching the sick being lifted into the boats You might have thought that he had little feeling, so stern and expressionless was his face, but once, when they raised a sufferer somewhat awkwardly and he groaned deeply, that rough man broke out all at once with an oath that was strangely like a prayer and bade the men, for God's sake, take more care. And, coming up to me, he clapped me on the shoulder, saying, "I am glad to see you here, old lady, among these poor fellows." I am most strangely deceived if I did not see a teardrop gathering in his eye.

It was on this same day, I think, that bending down over a poor fellow whose senses had quite gone and, I fear, would never return to him in this world, he took me for his wife and calling me "Mary, Mary," many times, asked me how it was he had got home so quickly and why he did not see the children and said he felt sure he should soon get better now.

Poor fellow! I could not undeceive him. I think the fancy happily caused by the touch of a woman's hand soothed his dying hour, for I do not fancy he could have lived to reach Scutari. I never knew it for certain, but I always felt sure that

he would never wake from that dream of home in this
world.

And here, lest the reader should consider that I am
speaking too highly of my own actions, I must have
recourse to a plan which I shall frequently adopt in the
following pages and let another voice speak for me in the
kind letter received long after Balaclava had been left to its
old masters, by one who had not forgotten his old
companion on the sickwharf. The writer, Major (then
Captain) R., had charge of the wharf while I was there.

Glasgow, Sept. 1856.

*DEAR MRS. SEACOLE — I am very sorry to hear that you
have been unfortunate in business, but I am glad to hear that you
have found friends in Lord R. and others, who are ready to help
you. No one knows better than I do how much you did to help poor
sick and wounded soldiers and I feel sure you will find in your day
of trouble that they have not forgotten it.*

Major R was a brave and experienced officer, but the scenes
on the sickwharf unmanned him often. I have known him
nervously restless if the people were behind-hand, even for
a few minutes, in their preparations for the wounded. But in
this feeling all shared alike. Only women could have done
more than they did who attended to this melancholy duty
and they, not because their hearts could be softer, but
because their hands are moulded for this work.

But it must not be supposed that we had no cheerful
scenes upon the sickwharf. Sometimes a light-hearted
follow — generally a sailor — would forget his pain and do
his best to keep the rest in good spirits. Once I heard my
name eagerly pronounced and turning round, recognised a

sailor whom I remembered as one of the crew of the *Alarm*, stationed at Kingston, a few years back.

"Why, as I live, if this ain't Aunty Seacole of Jamaica! Shiver all that's left of my poor timbers," I saw that his left leg was gone. "If this ain't a rum go, mates!"

"Ah, my man, I'm sorry to see you in this sad plight."

"Never fear for me, Aunty Seacole, I'll make the best of the leg the Russians have left me. I'll get at them soon again, never fear. You don't think, messmates," he never left his wounded comrades alone, "that they'll think less of us at home for coming back with a limb or so short?"

"You bear your troubles well, my son."

"Eh, do I, Aunty?" and he seemed surprised. "Why, look'ye, when I've seen so many pretty fellows knocked off the ship's roll altogether, don't you think I ought to be thankful if I can answer the bo'swain's call anyhow?"

And this was the sailors' philosophy always. And this brave fellow, after he had sipped some lemonade and laid down, when he heard the men groaning, raised his head and comforted them in the same strain again and, it may seem strange, but it quieted them.

I used to make spongecakes on board the *Medora*, with eggs brought from Constantinople. Only, the other day, Captain S., who had charge of the *Medora*, reminded me of them. These, with some lemonade, were all the doctors would allow me to give to the wounded. They all liked the cake, poor fellows, better than anything else. Perhaps because it tasted of home.

CHAPTER 11

My life in Balaclava could not but be a rough one. The exposure by day was enough to try any woman's strength and at night one was not always certain of repose. Nor was it the easiest thing to clamber up the steep sides of the *Medora*, and more than once I narrowly escaped a sousing in the harbour. Why it should be so difficult to climb a ship's side, when a few more staves in the ladder and those a little broader, would make it so easy, I have never been able to guess.

Once on board the *Medora*, my berth would not altogether have suited a delicate female with weak nerves. It was an ammunition ship and we slept over barrels of gunpowder and tons of cartridges, with the by no means impossible contingency of their prematurely igniting and giving us no time to say our prayers before launching us into eternity. Great care was enjoined and at eight o'clock every evening Captain S. would come down and order all lights out for the night. I used to put my lantern into a deep basin, behind some boxes and so evaded the regulation. I felt rather ashamed of this breach of discipline one night, when another ammunition ship caught fire in the crowded harbour and threatened us all with speedy destruction. We all knew, if they failed in extinguishing the fire pretty quickly, what our chances of life were worth and I think the bravest drew his breath heavily at the thought of our danger. Fortunately, they succeeded in extinguishing the firebrand before any mischief was done, but I do not think the crew of the *Medora* slept very comfortably that night. It was said that the Russians had employed an incendiary, but it would have been strange if in that densely crowded harbour some accidents had not happened without their agency.

Harassing work, indeed, was the getting our stores on shore, with the aid of the Greek and Maltese boatmen, whose profession is thievery. Not only did they demand exorbitant sums for the carriage, but they contrived to rob us by the way in the most ingenious manner. Thus many things of value were lost in the little journey from the *Albatross* and *Nonpareil* to the shore. Keep as sharp a look out as I might, some package or box would be tipped overboard by the sudden swaying of the boat, or passing by of one of the boatmen — of course, accidentally — and no words could induce the rascals, in their feigned ignorance of my language, to stop and, looking back at the helpless waif, it was not altogether consolatory to see another boat dart from between some shipping, where it had been waiting, as accidentally, ready to pounce upon any such wind or waterfalls.

Still more harassing work was it to keep the things together on the shore often in the open light of day, while I sat there (after my duties on the sickwharf were over) selling stores, or administering medicine to the men of the Land Transport and Army Works Corps and others, who soon found out my skill, valuable things would be abstracted, while there was no limit to the depredations by night. Of course we hired men to watch, but our choice of servants was very limited and very often those we employed not only shut their eyes to the plunder of their companions, but helped themselves freely. The adage, 'set a thief to catch a thief', answered very badly in Balaclava.

Sometimes Jew Johnny would volunteer to watch for the night and glad I was when I knew that the honest lynx-eyed fellow was there. One night he caught a great-limbed Turk making off with a firkin of butter and some other things. The fellow broke away from Johnny's grasp with the butter, but the lad marked him down to his wretched den, behind the engineers' quarters and, on the following morning, quietly introduced me to the lazy culprit, who was making up for the partial loss of his night's rest among as evil-looking a set of comrades as I have ever seen. There was a great row and much indignation shown at the purpose of my visit, but I considered myself justified in calling in the aid of one of the Provost Marshal's officers and, in the presence of this most invaluable official, a confession was soon made. Beneath the fellow's dirty bed, the butter was found buried and, in its company, a two dozen case of sherry, which the rogue had, in flagrant defiance of the Prophet's injunction, stolen for his own private drinking, a few nights previously.

The thievery in this little out of the way port was something marvellous and the skill and ingenuity of the operators would have reflected credit upon the elite of their profession practising in the most civilized city of Europe. Nor was the thievery confined altogether to the professionals who had crowded to this scene of action from the cities and islands of the Mediterranean. They robbed us, the Turks and one another, but a stronger hand was sometimes laid on them. The Turk, however, was sure to be the victim, let who might be the oppressor.

In this predatory warfare, as in more honourable service, the Zouaves particularly distinguished themselves. These undoubtedly gallant little fellows, always restless for action, of some sort, would, when the luxury of a brush with the Russians was occasionally denied them, come down to Balaclava, in search of opportunities of waging war against society at large. Their complete and utter absence of conscientious scruples as to the rights of property was most amusing. To see a Zouave gravely cheat a Turk, or trip up a Greek street merchant, or Maltese fruitseller and scud away with the spoil, cleverly stowed in his roomy red pantaloons, was an operation, for its coolness, expedition and perfectness, well worth seeing. And, to a great extent, they escaped scatheless, for the English Provost Marshal's department was rather wary of interfering with the eccentricities of our gallant allies, while if the French had taken close cognizance of the Zouaves' amusements out of school, one half of the regiments would have been always engaged punishing the other half.

The poor Turk! It is lamentable to think how he was robbed, abused and bullied by his friends. Why didn't he show a little pluck? There wasn't a rough sailor, or shrewd boy — the English boy, in all his impudence and prejudice, flourished in Balaclava — who would not gladly have patted him upon the back if he would but have held up his head and shown ever so little spirit. But the Englishman cannot understand a coward — will scarcely take the trouble to pity him and even the craven Greek could lord it over the degenerate descendants of the fierce Arabs, who — so they told me on the spot — had wrested Constantinople from the Christians, in those old times of which I know so little. Very often an injured Turk would run up to where I sat and stand there, wildly telegraphing his complaints against some villainous-looking Greek, or Italian, whom a stout English lad would have shaken out of his dirty skin in five minutes.

Once, however, I saw the tables turned. As the anecdote will help to illustrate the relative positions of the predatory tribes of Balaclava, I will narrate it.

Hearing one morning a louder hubbub than was usual upon the completion of a bargain and the inevitable quarrelling that always followed, I went up to where I saw an excited crowd collected around a Turk, in whose hands a Greek was struggling vainly. This Greek had, it seemed, robbed his enemy, but the Turk was master this time and had, in order to force from the robber a confession of the place where the stolen things were deposited (like dogs, as they were, these fellows were fond of burying their plunder), resorted to torture. This was effected most ingeniously and simply by means of some packthread which, bound round the Greek's two thumbs was tightened on the tourniquet principle, until the pain elicited a confession. But the Turk, stimulated to retaliation by his triumph, bagged the Greeks' basket, which contained amongst other things two watches, which their present owner had no doubt stolen. Driven to the most ludicrous show of despair, the Greek was about to attempt another desperate struggle for the recovery of his goods, when two Zouaves elbowed their small persons upon the crowded stage and were eagerly referred to by all the parties concerned in the squabble. How they contrived it, I cannot say, so prompt were their movements, but in a very few minutes, the watches were in their possession and going much faster than was agreeable either to Turk or Greek, who both combined to arrest this new movement and thereby added a sharp thrashing to their other injuries. The Zouaves effected their escape safely, while the Greek, with a despair that had in it an equal share of the ludicrous and the tragic, threw himself upon the dusty ground and tore his thin hair out by the handful. I believe that the poor wretch, whom we could not help pitying, journeyed to Kamiesch, to discover his oppressors, but I fear he didn't gain much information there.

Had it not been for the unremitting activity of the authorities, no life would have been safe in Balaclava, with its population of villains of every nation. As it was, murder was sometimes added to robbery and many of the rascals themselves died suspicious deaths with the particulars of which the authorities did not trouble themselves. But the officials worked hard, both in the harbour and on shore, to keep order, few men could have worked harder. I often saw the old grey-haired Admiral about before the sun had fairly shown itself and those of his subordinates must have been somewhat heavy sleepers who could play the sluggard then.

At length the necessary preparations to establish our store were made. We hit upon a spot about two miles from Balaclava, in advance of Kadikoi, close to where the railway engines were stationed and within a mile of headquarters. Leave having been obtained to erect buildings here, we set to work briskly and soon altered the appearance of Spring Hill — so we christened our new home.

Sometimes on horseback, sometimes getting a lift on the commissariat carts and occasionally on the ammunition railway wagons, I managed to visit Spring Hill daily and very soon fitted up a shed sufficiently large to take up my abode in. But the difficulty of building our store was immense. To obtain material was next to impossible, but that collected (not a little was, by leave of the Admiral, gleaned from the floating rubbish in the harbour), to find workmen to make use of it was still more difficult. I spent days going round the shipping, offering great wages, even for an invalid able to handle saw and hammer, however roughly and many a long ride through the camps did I take on the same errand. At length, by dint of hard canvassing, we obtained the aid of two English sailors, whom nicknamed 'Big and Little Chips', and some Turks and set to work in good earnest.

I procured the Turks from the Pacha who commanded the division encamped in the neighbourhood of Spring Hill. It was decided that we should apply to him for help and accordingly I became ambassadress on this delicate mission and rode over to the Pacha's quarters.

Jew Johnny attending me as interpreter, I was received by the Pacha with considerable kindness and no trifling amount of formality. After taking coffee I proceeded, through Jew Johnny, to explain the object of my visit, while his excellency, a tall man, with a dark pleasing face, smoked gravely and took my request into his gracious consideration.

On the following day came the answer to my request, in the persons of two curious Turkish carpenters, who were placed at our orders. After a little while, too, a Turkish officer, whom I christened Captain Ali Baba, took so great an interest in our labours that he would work like any carpenter and with a delight and zeal that were astonishing. To see him fall back and look smilingly at every piece of his workmanship, was a sight to restore the most severely tried temper. I really think that the good-hearted fellow thought it splendid fun and never wearied of it. But for him I do not know how we should have managed with our other Turkish 'chips' — chips off the true old Turkish block they were — deliberate, slow and indolent, breaking off into endless interruptions for the sacred duties of eating and praying and getting into out of the way corners at all times of the day to smoke themselves to sleep.

In the midst of our work a calamity occurred which was very nearly becoming a catastrophe. By the giving way of a dam, after some heavy rains, the little stream which threaded its silvery way past Spring Hill swelled without any warning into a torrent which, sweeping through my temporary hut, very nearly carried us all away and destroyed stores of between one and two hundred pounds in value. This calamity might have had a tragical issue for me, for seeing a little box which contained some things, valuable as relics of the past, being carried away, I plunged in after it and, losing my balance, was rolled over and over by the stream and with some difficulty reached the shore.

Some of Lord Raglan's staff passing our wreck on the following day, made inquiries respecting the loss we had sustained and a messenger was sent from headquarters, who made many purchases, in token of their sympathy.

My visit to the Turkish Pacha laid the foundation of a lasting friendship. He soon found his way to Spring Hill and before long became one of my best customers and most frequent visitors. It was astonishing to note how completely, now that he was in the land of these Giaours, he adapted himself to the tastes and habits of the infidels. Like a Scotch Presbyterian, on the Continent for a holiday, he threw aside all the prejudices of his education and drank bottled beer, sherry and champagne with an appreciation of their qualities that no thirsty-souled Christian could have expressed more gratefully. He was very affable with us all and would sometimes keep Jew Johnny away from his work for hours, chatting with us or the English officers who would lounge into our as yet unfinished store. Sometimes he would come down to breakfast and spend the greater part of the day at Spring Hill. Indeed, the wits of Spring Hill used to laugh and say that the crafty Pacha was throwing his pocket handkerchief at Madame Seacole, widow, but as the honest fellow candidly confessed he had three wives already at home, I acquit him of any desire to add to their number.

The Pacha's great ambition was to be familiar with the English language and at last nothing would do but he must take lessons from me. So he would come down and, sitting in my store with a Turk or two at his feet to attend to his most important pipe by inserting little red-hot pieces of charcoal at intervals, would try hard to store a few English sentences in his treacherous memory. He never got beyond half a dozen and I think if we had continued in the relation of pupil and mistress until now, the number would not have been increased greatly. "Madame Seacole," "Gentlemen, good morning," and "More champagne," with each syllable much dwelt upon, were his favourite sentences. It was capital fun to hear him, when I was called away suddenly to attend to a customer, or to give a sick man medicine, repeating gravely the sentence we had been studying, until I passed him and started him with another.

Very frequently he would compliment me by ordering his band down to Spring Hill for my amusement. They played excellently well and I used to think that I preferred their music to that of the French and English regimental bands. I laughed heartily one day when, in compliance with the kind-hearted Anglo-Turkish Pacha's orders, they came out with a grand new tune, in which I with difficulty recognised a very distant resemblance to *God save the Queen*.

Altogether he was a capital neighbour and gave such strict orders to his men to respect our property that we rarely lost anything. On the whole, the Turks were the most honest of the nations there (except the English and the Sardinians) and the most tractable.

But the Greeks hated them and showed their hate in every way. In bringing up things for the Pacha's use they would let the mules down and smash their loads most relentlessly. Now and then they suffered, as was the case one day when I passed through the camp and saw my friend superintending the correction of a Greek who was being bastinadoed. It seemed a painful punishment.

I was sorry, therefore, when my friend's division was ordered to Kamara and we lost our neighbours. But my pupil did not forget his schoolmistress. A few days after they had left the neighbourhood of Spring Hill came a messenger, with a present of lambs, poultry, eggs and a letter, which I could not decipher, as many of the interpreters could speak English far better than they could write it. But we discovered that the letter contained an invitation, to Mr. Day and myself, to go over to Kamara and select from the spoil of the village anything that might be useful in our new buildings. And a few days later came over a large araba, drawn by four mules and laden with a pair of glass doors and some window frames, which the thoughtful kind Pacha had judged — and judged rightly — would be a very acceptable present. And very often the good-natured fellow would ride over from Kamara and resume his acquaintance with myself and my champagne and practice his English sentences.

We felt the loss of our Turkish neighbours in more ways than one. The neighbourhood, after their departure, was left lonely and unprotected and it was not until a division of the Land Transport Corps came and took up their quarters near us, that I felt at all secure of personal safety. Mr. Day rarely returned to Spring Hill until nightfall relieved him from his many duties and I depended chiefly upon two sailors, both of questionable character, two black servants, Jew Johnny and my own reputation for determination and courage — a poor delusion, which I took care to heighten by the judicious display of a double-barrelled pistol, lent me for the purpose by Mr. Day and which I couldn't have loaded to save my life.

CHAPTER 12

Summer was fairly advanced before the British Hotel was anything like finished. Indeed, it never was completed and when we left the Hill, a year later, it still wanted shutters. But long before that time Spring Hill had gained a great reputation. Of course, I have nothing to do with what occurred in the camp, although I could not help hearing a great deal about it. Mismanagement and privation there might have been, but my business was to make things right in my sphere and, whatever confusion and disorder existed elsewhere, comfort and order were always to be found at Spring Hill.

When there was no sun elsewhere, some few gleams — so its grateful visitors said — always seemed to have stayed behind, to cheer the weary soldiers that gathered in the British Hotel. And, perhaps, as my kind friend *Punch* said, after all these things had become pleasant memories of the past:

> The cold without gave a zest, no doubt, To the
> welcome warmth within
> But her smile, good old soul, lent heat to the
> coal and power to the pannikin.

Let me, in a few words, describe the British Hotel. It was acknowledged by all to be the most complete thing there. It cost no less than £800. The buildings and yards took up at least an acre of ground and were as perfect as we could make them. The hotel and storehouse consisted of a long iron room with counters closets and shelves, above it was another low room, used by us for storing our goods and above this floated a large Union Jack. Attached to this building was a little kitchen, not unlike a ship's caboose — all stoves and shelves. In addition to the iron house were two wooden houses, with sleeping apartments for myself and Mr. Day, outhouses for our servants, a canteen for the soldiery and a large enclosed yard for our stock, full of stables, low huts and sties. Everything, although rough and unpolished, was comfortable and warm and there was a completeness about the whole which won general admiration. The reader may judge of the manner in which we had stocked the interior of our store from the remark, often repeated by the officers, that you might get everything at Mother Seacole's, from an anchor down to a needle.

In addition, we had for our transport service four carts and as many horses and mules as could be kept from the thieves. To reckon upon being in possession of these, at any future time, was impossible, we have more than once seen a fair stud stabled at night time and on the following morning been compelled to borrow cattle from the Land Transport camp, to fetch our things up from Balaclava.

But it must not be supposed that my domestic difficulties came to an end with the completion of the hotel. True, I was in a better position to bear the Crimean cold and rain, but my other foes were as busy as ever they had been on the beach at Balaclava. Thieves, biped and quadruped, human and animal, troubled me more than ever and perhaps the most difficult to deal with were the least dangerous. The

Crimean rats, for instance, who had the appetites of London aldermen and were as little dainty as hungry schoolboys. Whether they had left Sebastopol, guided by the instinct which leads their kindred in other parts of the world to forsake sinking ships, or because the garrison rations offended their palates, or whether they had patriotically emigrated, to make war against the English larders, I do not pretend to guess, but whatever was their motive, it drew them in great abundance to Spring Hill. They occasionally did us damage, in a single night, to the tune of two or three pounds — wasting what they could not devour. You could keep nothing sacred from their strong teeth. When hard pressed they more than once attacked the live sheep and eventually went so far as to nibble one of our black cooks, Francis, who slept among the flour barrels. On the following morning he came to me, his eyes rolling angrily and his white teeth gleaming, to show me a mangled finger, which they had bitten, and asked me to dress it. He made a great fuss and a few mornings later he came in a violent passion this time and gave me instant notice to quit my service, although we were paying him two pounds a week, with board and rations. This time the rats had, it appeared, been bolder and attacked his head, in a spot where its natural armour, the woolly hair, was thinnest and the silly fellow had a notion that the souls of the slain Russian soldiers had entered the bodies of the rats and made vengeful war upon their late enemies. Driven to such an extremity I made up my mind to scour the camp in search of a cat and, after a long day's hunt, I came to the conclusion that the tale of Whittington was by no means an improbable one. Indeed, had a brisk young fellow with a cat, of even ordinary skill in its profession, made their appearance at Spring Hill, I would gladly have put them in the way of laying the foundation, at least of a fortune.

At last I found a benefactor, in the Guards' camp, in Colonel D., of the Coldstreams, who kindly promised me a great pet, well known in the camp and perhaps by some who may read these pages, by the name of Pinkie. Pinkie was then helping a brother officer to clear his hut, but on the following day a Guardsman brought the noble fellow down. He lived in clover for a few days, but he had an English cat-like attachment for his old house and, despite the abundance of game, Pinkie soon stole away to his old master's quarters, three miles away. More than once the men brought him back to me, but the attractions of Spring Hill were never strong enough to detain him long with me.

From the human thieves that surrounded Spring Hill, I had to stand as sharp a siege as the Russians had in that poor city against which we heard the guns thundering daily, while the most cunning and desperate sorties were often made upon the most exposed parts of my defences and sometimes with success. Scores of the keenest eyes and hundreds of the sharpest fingers in the world were always ready to take advantage of the least oversight. I had to keep two boys, whose chief occupation was to watch the officers' horses, tied up to the doorposts of the British Hotel. Before I adopted this safeguard, more than one officer would leave his horse for a few minutes and on his return find it gone to the neighbourhood of the Naval Brigade, or the horsefair at Kamiesch. My old friends, the Zouaves, soon found me out at Spring Hill and the wiry, light-fingered, fighting, loving gentry spent much of their leisure there. Those confounded trousers of theirs offered conveniences of storage room which they made use of. Nothing was too small and few things too unwieldy, to ride in them, like the pockets of a clown in a pantomime, they could accommodate a well-grown baby or a pound of sausages equally well. I have a firm conviction that they stuffed turkeys, geese and fowls into them and I positively know that my only respectable teapot travelled off in the same conveyance, while I detected one little fellow, who had tied them down tight at his ankles, stowing away some pounds of tea and coffee mixed. Some officers, who were present, cut the cords and, holding up the little scamp by the neck, shook his trousers empty amid shouts of laughter.

Our livestock, from the horses and mules down to the geese and fowls, suffered terribly. Although we kept a sharp lookout by day and paid a man five shillings a night as watchman, our losses were very great. During the time we were in the Crimea we lost over a score of horses, four mules, eighty goats, many sheep, pigs and poultry, by thieving alone. We missed in a single night forty goats and seven sheep and, on Mr. Day's going to headquarters with intelligence of the disaster, they told him that Lord Raglan had recently received forty sheep from Asia, all of which had disappeared in the same manner. The geese, turkeys and fowls vanished by scores. We found out afterwards that the watchman paid to guard the sheep, used to kill a few occasionally. As he represented them to have died a natural death during the night, he got permission to bury them, instead of which he sold them.

King Frost claimed his share of our stock too and on one December night, of the winter of 1855, killed no less than forty sheep. It is all very well to smile at these things now, but at the time they were heart-rending enough and helped, if they did not cause, the ruin which eventually overtook the firm of Seacole and Day. The determination and zeal which besiegers and besieged showed with respect to a poor pig, which was quietly and unconsciously fattening in its sty, are worthy of record.

Fresh pork, in the spring of 1856, was certainly one of those luxuries not easily obtainable in that part of the Crimea to which the British army was confined and when it became known that Mother Seacole had purchased a promising young porker from one of the ships in Balaclava and that, brave woman, she had formed the courageous resolution of fattening it for her favourites, the excitement among the frequenters of Spring Hill was very great. I could laugh heartily now, when I think of the amount of persuasion and courting I stood out for before I bound myself how its four legs were to be disposed of. I learnt more at that time of the trials and privileges of authority than I am ever likely to experience again. Upon my word, I think if the poor thing had possessed as many legs as my editor tells me somebody called the Hydra (with whom my readers are perhaps more familiar than I am) had heads, I should have found candidates for them. As it was, the contest for those I had to bestow was very keen and the lucky individuals who were favoured by me looked after their interests most carefully. One of them, to render mistake or misunderstanding impossible, entered the promise in my daybook. The reader will perhaps smile at the following important memorandum in the gallant officer's writing:

Memorandum that Mrs. Seacole did this day, in the presence of Major A. and Lieutenant W., promise Captain H., a leg of the pig.

Now it was well known that many greedy eyes and fingers were directed towards the plump fellow and considerable interest was manifested in the result of the struggle, 'Mrs. Seacole versus Thievery'. I think they had some confidence in me and that I was the favourite, but there was a large field against me, which found its backers also and many a bet was laughingly laid on the ultimate fate of the unconscious porker.

I baffled many a knavish trick to gain possession of the fine fellow but, after all, I lost him in the middle of the day, when I thought the boldest rogues would not have run the risk. The shouts and laughter of some officers who were riding down from the front first informed me of my loss. Up they rode, calling out, "Mother Seacole! Old lady! Quick! The pig's gone!"

I rushed out, injured woman that I was and saw it all at a glance. But that my straw wide awake was in the way, I could have torn my hair in my vexation. I rushed to the sty, found the nest warm and with prompt decision prepared for speedy pursuit. Back I came to the horsemen, calling out, "Off with you, my sons, they can't have got very far away yet. Do your best to save my bacon!"

Delighted with the fun, the horsemen dispersed, laughing and shouting, "Stole away! Hark away!" while I ran indoors, turned out all my available bodyguards and started in pursuit also. Not half a mile off we soon saw a horseman wave his cap and, starting off into a run, came to a little hollow, where the poor panting animal and two Greek thieves had been run down. The Provost Marshal took the latter in hand willingly and piggy was brought home in triumph. But those who had pork expectancies, hearing of the adventure, grew so seriously alarmed at the narrow escape, that they petitioned me to run so desperate a hazard no longer and the poor thing was killed on the following day and distributed according to promise. A certain portion was reserved for sausages which, fried with mashed potatoes, were quite the rage at the British Hotel for some days. Some pork was also sent to headquarters, with an account of the dangers we ran from thieves. It drew the following kind acknowledgment from General B.:

> *Headquarters*
> *MY DEAR MRS. SEACOLE, I am very much obliged to you indeed for your pork. I have spoken to Colonel P. as to the police of your neighbourhood and he will see what arrangement can be made for the general protection of that line of road. When the highroad is finished, you will be better off. Let me know at the time of any depredations that are committed and we will try and protect you.*
> *I am, faithfully yours*
> *M. L. B.*

For the truth was — although I can laugh at my fears now — I was often most horribly frightened at Spring Hill and there was cause for it too. My washerwoman who, with her family, lived not half a mile from us, was with me one day and carried off some things for the wash. On the following morning I was horrified to learn that she, her father, husband and children — in all, seven — had been most foully murdered during the night. Only one of the whole family recovered from her wounds and lived to tell the tale. It created a great sensation at the time and caused me to pass many a sleepless night, for the murderers were never discovered.

Whilst I am upon the subject of Crimean thievery, I may as well exhaust it without paying any regard to the chronological order of my reminiscences.

I have before mentioned what I suffered from the French. One day I caught one of our allies in my kitchen, robbing me in the most ungrateful manner. He had met with an accident near Spring Hill (I believe he belonged to a French regiment lent to assist the English in roadmaking) and had been doctored by me and now I found him filling his pockets, before taking 'French' leave of us. My black man, Francis, pulled from his pockets a yet warm fowl and other provisions. We kicked him off the premises and he found refuge with some men of the Army Works Corps, who pitied him and gave him shelter. He woke them in the middle of the night, laying hands rather clumsily on everything that was removable and in the morning they brought him to me, to ask what they should do with him. Unluckily for him, a French officer of rank happened to be in the store, who, on hearing our tale, packed him off to his regiment. I gathered from the expression on the officer's face and the dread legible upon the culprit's, that it might be some considerable time before his itch for breaking the eighth commandment could be again indulged in.

The trouble I underwent respecting a useful black mare, for which Mr. Day had given thirty guineas and which carried me beautifully, was immense. Before it had been many weeks in our store it was gone — whither, I failed to discover. Keeping my eyes wide open, however, I saw 'Angelina' — so I christened her — coming quietly down the hill, carrying an elderly naval officer. I was ready to receive the unconscious couple and soon made my claim good. Of course, the officer was not to blame. He had bought it from a sailor, who in his turn had purchased the animal of a messmate, who of course had obtained it from another and so on, but eventually it returned to its old quarters, where it only remained about a fortnight. I grew tired of looking for Angelina and had given her up, when one day she turned up, in capital condition, in the possession of a French officer of Chasseurs. But nothing I could say to the Frenchman would induce him to take the view of the matter I wished, but had no right to enforce. He had bought the horse at Kamiesch and intended to keep it. We grew hot at last and our dispute drew out so large an audience that the Frenchman took alarm and tried to make off. I held on to Angelina for a little while, but at last the mare broke away from me and vanished in a cloud of dust. It was the last I ever saw of Angelina.

More than once the Crimean thievery reduced us to woeful straits. To a Greek, returning to Constantinople, we entrusted (after the murder of our washerwoman) two trunks, containing things for the wash, which he was to bring back as soon as possible. But neither upon Greek, trunks, nor their contents did we ever set eyes again. It was a serious loss. The best part of our tablecloths and other domestic linen, all my clothes, except two suits and all of Mr. Day's linen vanished and had to be replaced as best we could by fresh purchases from Kamiesch and Kadikoi.

Perhaps the most ridiculous shift I was ever put to by the Crimean thieves happened when we rose one morning and found the greater part of our stud missing. I had, in the course of the day, urgent occasion to ride over to the French camp on the Tchernaya, the only animal available for my transport was an old grey mare, who had contracted some equine disease of which I do not know the name, but which

gave her considerable resemblance to a dog suffering from
the mange. Now, go to the French camp I must, to borrow a
horse was impossible and something must be done with the
grey. Suddenly one of those happy thoughts which
sometimes help us over our greatest difficulties entered into
my scheming brains. Could I not conceal the poor mare's
worst blemishes? Her colour was grey, would not a thick
coating of flour from my dredger make all right? There was
no time to be lost, the remedy was administered
successfully and off I started. Alas, the wind was high and
swept the skirts of my riding habit so determinedly against
the side of the poor beast, that before long its false coat was
transferred to the dark cloth and my innocent ruse exposed.
The French are proverbially and really a polite and
considerate nation, but I never heard more hearty peals of
laughter from any sides than those which conveyed to me
the horrible assurance that my scheme had unhappily
failed.

CHAPTER 13

I hope the reader will give me credit for the assertion that I am about to make: I enter upon the particulars of this chapter with great reluctance, but I cannot omit them, for the simple reason that they strengthen my one and only claim to interest the public, viz., my services to the brave British army in the Crimea.

But, fortunately, I can follow a course which will not only render it unnecessary for me to sound my own trumpet, but will be more satisfactory to the reader. I can put on record the written opinions of those who had ample means of judging and ascertaining how I fulfilled the great object which I had in view when leaving England for the Crimea. Before I do so, I must solicit my readers' attention to the position I held in the camp as doctress, nurse and 'mother'.

I have never been long in any place before I have found my practical experience in the science of medicine useful. When in London I have found it of service to others and, in the Crimea, where the doctors were so overworked and sickness was so prevalent, I could not be long idle, for I never forgot that my intention in seeking the army was to help the kind-hearted doctors, to be useful to whom I have ever looked upon and still regard as so high a privilege.

But before very long I found myself surrounded with patients of my own and this for two simple reasons. In the first place, the men (I am speaking of the 'ranks' now) had a very serious objection to going into hospital for any but urgent reasons and the regimental doctors were rather fond of sending them there. In the second place, they could and did get at my store sick comforts and nourishing food, which the heads of the medical staff would sometimes find it difficult to procure. These reasons, with the additional one that I was very familiar with the diseases which they suffered most from and successful in their treatment (I say this in no spirit of vanity), were quite sufficient to account for the numbers who came daily to the British Hotel for medical treatment.

That the officers were glad of me as a doctress and nurse may be easily understood. When a poor fellow lay sickening in his cheerless hut and sent down to me, he knew very well that I should not answer his needs empty-handed. Although I did not hesitate to charge him with the value of the necessaries I took him, still he was thankful enough to be able to purchase them. When we lie ill at home surrounded with comfort, we never think of feeling any special gratitude for the sick room delicacies which we accept as a consequence of our illness, but the poor officer lying ill and weary in his hut, dependent for the merest necessaries of existence upon a clumsy, ignorant soldier cook, who would almost prefer eating his meat raw to having the trouble of cooking it (our English soldiers are bad campaigners), often finds his greatest troubles in the want of those little delicacies with which a weak stomach must be humoured into retaining nourishment. How often have I felt sad at the sight of poor lads who in England thought attending early parade a hardship and felt harassed if their neckcloths sat awry, or the natty little boots would not retain their polish, bearing and bearing so nobly and bravely, trials and hardships to which the veteran campaigner frequently succumbed. Don't you think, reader, if you were lying, with parched lips and fading appetite, thousands of miles from mother, wife, or sister, loathing the rough food by your side and thinking regretfully of that English home where nothing that could minister to your great need would be left untried — don't you think that you would welcome the familiar figure of the stout lady whose bony horse has just pulled up at the door of your hut and whose panniers contain some cooling drink, a little broth, some homely cake, or a dish of jelly or blancmange. Don't you think, under such circumstances, that you would heartily agree with my friend *Punch's* remark:

> *That berry brown face, with a kind heart's*
> *trace*
> *Impressed on each wrinkle sly,*
> *Was a sight to behold, through the snow*
> *clouds rolled*
> *Across that iron sky.*

I tell you, reader, I have seen many a bold fellow's eyes moisten at such a season, when a woman's voice and a woman's care have brought to their minds recollections of those happy English homes which some of them never saw again, but many did, who will remember their woman comrade upon the bleak and barren heights before Sebastopol.

Then their calling me "mother" was not, I think, altogether unmeaning. I used to fancy that there was something homely in the word and, reader, you cannot think how dear to them was the smallest thing that reminded them of home.

Some of my Crimean patients who were glad of me as nurse and doctress, bore names familiar to all England and perhaps, if I asked them, they would allow me to publish those names. I am proud to think that a gallant sailor, on whose brave breast the order of Victoria rests — a more gallant man can never wear it — sent for the doctress whom he had known in Kingston, when his arm, wounded on the fatal 18th of June, refused to heal and I think that the application I recommended did it good, but I shall let some of my patients' letters, taken from a large bundle, speak for me. Of course I must suppress most of their names. Here are two from one of my best and kindest sons.

MY DEAR MRS. SEACOLE
Will you kindly give the bearer the bottle you promised me when you were here this morning, for my jaundice. Please let me know how much I am to take of it.
Yours truly
F. M.

You see the medicine does him good, for a few days later comes another from the same writer.

MY DEAR MRS. SEACOLE
I have finished the bottle, which has done my jaundice a deal of good. Will you kindly send another by bearer.
Truly yours
F. M.

It was a capital prescription which had done his jaundice good. There was so great a demand for it, that I kept it mixed in a large pan, ready to ladle it out to the scores of applicants who came for it.

Sometimes they would send for other and no less important medicines. Here is such an application from a sick officer.

Mrs. Seacole would confer a favour on the writer, who is very ill, by giving his servant (the bearer) a boiled or roast fowl, if it be impossible to obtain, then some chicken broth would be very acceptable.

I am yours, truly obliged

J. K, 18th R. S.

Here is a certificate from one of the Army Works' men, to whose case I devoted no little time and trouble.

I certify that I was labouring under a severe attack of diarrhoea last August and that I was restored to health through the instrumentality and kindness of Mrs. Seacole.

I also certify that my fingers were severely jammed whilst at work at Frenchman's Hill and Mrs. Seacole cured me after three doctors had fruitlessly attempted to care them.

I cannot leave the Crimea without testifying to the kindness and skill of Mrs. Seacole and may God reward her for it.

JAMES WALLEN

5th Division Army Works Corps

Here is a letter from a civilian.

Upper Clapton, Middlesex, March 2, 1866.

DEAR MADAM

Having been informed by my son, Mr. Edward Gill, of St. George's Store, Crimea, of his recent illness (jaundice) and of your kind attention and advice to him during that illness and up to the time he was, by the blessing of God and your assistance, restored to health, permit me, on behalf of myself, my wife and my family, to return you our most grateful thanks, trusting you may be spared for many years to come, in health of body and of mind, to carry out your benevolent intention.

Believe me, my dear madam, yours most gratefully,
EDWARD GILL

And now that I have made this a chapter of testimonials, I may as well finish them right off and have done with them altogether. I shall trouble the patient reader with three more only, which I have not the heart to omit.

Sebastopol, July 1, 1866
Mrs. Seacole was with the British army in the Crimea from February, 1855, to this time. This excellent woman has frequently exerted herself in the most praiseworthy manner in attending wounded men, even in positions of great danger and in assisting sick soldiers by all means in her power. In addition, she kept a very good store and supplied us with many comforts at a time we much required them.
Wm. P.
Adjutant General of the British Army in the Crimea.

The second is from the pen of one who at that time was more looked to and better known than any other man in the Crimea. In the 2nd vol. of Russell's *Letters from the Seat of War*, p. 187, is the following entry:

In the hour of their illness these men (Army Works Corps), in common with many others, have found a kind and successful physician. Close to the railway, halfway between the Col de Balaclava and Kadikoi, Mrs. Seacole, formerly of Kingston and of several other parts of the world, such as Panama and Chagres, has pitched her abode — an iron storehouse with wooden sheds and outlying tributaries — and here she doctors and cures all manner of men with extraordinary success. She is always in attendance near the battlefield to aid the wounded and has earned many a poor fellow's blessings.

Yes! I cannot — referring to that time — conscientiously charge myself with doing less for the men who had only thanks to give me, than for the officers whose gratitude gave me the necessaries of life. I think I was ever ready to turn from the latter to help the former, humble as they might be and they were grateful in their way and as far as they could be. They would buy me apples and other fruit at Balaclava and leave them at my store. One made me promise, when I returned home, to send word to his Irish mother, who was to send me a cow in token of her gratitude for the help I had been to her son. I have a book filled with hundreds of the names of those who came to me for medicines and other aids and never a train of sick or wounded men from the front passed the British Hotel but its hostess was awaiting them to offer comforts to the poor fellows, for whose suffering her heart bled.

Punch, who allowed my poor name to appear in the pages which had welcomed Miss Nightingale home — *Punch*, that whimsical mouthpiece of some of the noblest hearts that ever beat beneath black coats — shall last of all raise its voice, that never yet pleaded an unworthy cause, for the Mother Seacole that takes shame to herself for speaking thus of the poor part she bore of the trials and hardships endured on that distant shore, where Britain's best and bravest wrung hardly Sebastopol from the grasp of Britain's foe:

No store she set by the epaulette
Be it worsted or gold lace
For K. C. B. or plain private Smith
She had still one pleasant face.

And not alone was her kindness shown
To the bale and hungry lot
Who drank her grog and ate her prog and
paid their honest shot.

The sick and sorry can tell the story
Of her nursing and dosing deeds,
Regimental M.D. never worked as she
In helping sick men's needs.

Of such work, God knows, was as much as she
chose
That dreary wintertide
When Death hung over the damp and
pestilent camp and his scythe swung far and
wide.

She gave her aid to all who prayed
To hungry and sick and cold
Open hand and heart, alike ready to part
Kind words and acts and gold.
And be the right man in the right place who can
The right woman was Dame Seacole.

CHAPTER 14

I shall proceed in this chapter to make the reader acquainted with some of the customers of the British Hotel, who came there for its creature comforts as well as its hostess's medicines when need was, and if he or she should be inclined to doubt or should hesitate at accepting my experience of Crimean life as entirely credible, I beg that individual to refer to the accounts which were given in the newspapers of the spring of 1855 and I feel sure they will acquit me of any intention to exaggerate. If I were to speak of all the nameless horrors of that spring as plainly as I could, I should really disgust you, but those I shall bring before your notice have all something of the humorous in them — and so it ever is. Time is a great restorer and hangs surely the greatest sorrow into an easing memory.

The sun shines this springtime upon green grass that covers the graves of the poor fellows we left behind sadly a few short months ago. Bright flowers grow upon ruins of batteries and crumbling trenches, and cover the sod that presses on many a mouldering token of the old time of battle and death. I dare say that, if I went to the Crimea now, I should see a smiling landscape, instead of the bloodstained scene which I shall ever associate with distress and death and as it is with nature so it is with human kind. Whenever I meet those who have survived that dreary spring of 1855, we seldom talk about its horrors, but remembering its transient gleams of sunshine, smile at the fun and good nature that varied its long and weary monotony. And now that I am anxious to remember all I can that will interest my readers, my memory prefers to dwell upon what was pleasing and amusing, although the time will never come when it will cease to retain most vividly the pathos and woe of those dreadful months.

I have said that the winter had not ended when we began operations at the British Hotel and very often, after we considered we were fairly under spring's influence, our old enemy would come back with an angry roar of wind and rain, levelling tents, unroofing huts, destroying roads and handing over May to the command of General Fevrier. But the sun fought bravely for us and in time always dispersed the leaden clouds and gilded the iron sky and made us cheerful again.

During the end of March, the whole of April and a considerable portion of May, however, the army was but a little better off for the advent of spring. The military road to the camp was only in progress — the railway only carried ammunition. A few hours' rain rendered the old road all but impassable and scarcity often existed in the front before Sebastopol, although the frightened and anxious Commissariat toiled hard to avert such a mishap, so that very often to the British Hotel came officers starved out on the heights above us. The dandies of Rotten Row would come down riding on sorry nags, ready to carry back — their servants were on duty in the trenches — anything that would be available for dinner. A single glance at their personal appearance would suffice to show the hardships of the life they were called upon to lead. Before I left London for the seat of war I had been more than once to the United

Service Club, seeking to gain the interest of officers whom I had known in Jamaica and I often thought afterwards of the difference between those I saw there trimly shaven, handsomely dressed, with spotless linen and dandy air, and these their companions, who in England would resemble them. Roughly, warmly dressed, with great fur caps, which met their beards and left nothing exposed but lips and nose and not much of those, you would easily believe that soap and water were luxuries not readily obtainable, that shirts and socks were often comforts to dream about rather than possess and that they were familiar with horrors you would shudder to hear named. Tell me, reader, can you fancy what the want of so simple a thing as a pocket handkerchief is? To put a case — have you ever gone out for the day without one, sat in a draught and caught a sneezing cold in the head? You say the question is an unnecessarily unpleasant one and yet what I am about to tell you is true and the sufferer is, I believe, still alive.

An officer had ridden down one day to obtain refreshments (this was very early in the spring), some nice fowls had just been taken from the spit and I offered one to him. Paper was one of the most hardly obtainable luxuries of the Crimea and I rarely had any to waste upon my customers, so I called out, "Give me your pocket handkerchief, my son, that I may wrap it up." You see, he could not be very particular out there. But he smiled very bitterly as he answered, "Pocket handkerchief, mother? By Jove, I wish I had one. I tore my last shirt into shreds a fortnight ago and there's not a bit of it left now."

Shortly after, a hundred dozen pocket handkerchiefs came to my store and I sold them all to officers and men very speedily.

For some time and until I found the task beyond my strength, I kept up a capital table at the British Hotel, but at last I gave up doing so and my hungry customers had to make do with whatever was on the premises. Fortunately they were not over dainty and had few antipathies. My duties increased so rapidly, that sometimes it was with difficulty that I found time to eat and sleep. Could I have obtained good servants, my daily labours would have been lightened greatly, but my staff never consisted of more than a few boys, two black cooks, some Turks — one of whom, Osman, had enough to do to kill and pluck the poultry, while the others looked after the stock and killed our goats and sheep — and as many runaway sailors or good-for-noughts in search of employment as we could from time to time lay our hands upon, but they never found my larder entirely empty. I often used to roast a score or so of fowls daily, besides boiling hams and tongues. Either these or a slice from a joint of beef or mutton you would be pretty sure of finding at your service in the larder of the British Hotel.

Would you like, gentle reader, to know what other things suggestive of home and its comforts your relatives and friends in the Crimea could obtain from the hostess of Spring Hill? I do not tell you that the following articles were all obtainable at the commencement, but many were. The time was indeed when, had you asked me for mock turtle and venison, you should have had them preserved in tins, but that was when the Crimea was flooded with plenty. Too late, alas, to save many whom want had killed, but had you been doing your best to batter Sebastopol about the ears of the Russians in the spring and summer of the year before last, the firm of Seacole and Day would have been happy to have served you with linen and hosiery, saddlery, caps, boots and shoes, for the outer man and for the inner man, meat and soups of every variety in tins (you can scarcely conceive how disgusted we all became at last with preserved provisions), salmon, lobsters and oysters, also in tins, which was beaten up into fritters, with onions, butter, eggs, pepper and salt. There were very good game, wildfowl, vegetables, also preserved, eggs, sardines, curry powder, cigars, tobacco, cigarette papers, tea, coffee, tooth powder and currant jelly. When cargoes came in from Constantinople we bought great supplies of potatoes, carrots, turnips and greens. Ah, what a rush there used to be for the greens. You might sometimes get hot rolls but, generally speaking, I bought the Turkish bread baked at Balaclava.

Or had you felt too ill to partake of your rough camp fire food, coarsely cooked by a soldier who, unlike the French, could turn his hand to few things but fighting, and had ridden down that muddy road to the Col, to see what Mother Seacole could give you for dinner, the chances were you would have found a good joint of mutton (not of the fattest, forsooth, for in such miserable condition were the poor beasts landed, that once, when there came an urgent order from headquarters for twenty five pounds of mutton, we had to cut up one sheep and a half to provide the quantity), or you would have stumbled upon something curried, or upon a good Irish stew, nice and hot, with plenty of onions and potatoes. Or upon some capital meat pies. I found the preserved meats were better relished cooked in this fashion and well-doctored with stimulants.

Before long I grew as familiar with the mysteries of seasoning as any London pieman and could accommodate myself to the requirements of the seasons as readily.

Or had there been nothing better, you might have gone further and fared on worse fare than one of my Welsh rabbits, for the manufacture of which I became so famous. And had you been fortunate enough to have visited the British Hotel upon rice pudding day, I warrant you would have ridden back to your hut with kind thoughts of Mother Seacole's endeavours to give you a taste of home.

If I had nothing else to be proud of, I think my rice puddings, made without milk, upon the high road to Sebastopol, would have gained me a reputation. What a shout there used to be when I came out of my little caboose, hot and curried and called out, "Rice pudding day, my sons."

Some of them were baked in large shallow pads, for the men and the sick who always said that it reminded them of home.

You would scarcely expect to finish up your dinner with pastry, but very often you would have found a good stock of it in my larder. Whenever I had a few leisure moments, I used to wash my hands, roll up my sleeves and roll out pastry. Very often I was interrupted to dispense medicines, but if the tarts had a flavour of senna, or the paddings tasted of rhubarb, it never interfered with their consumption.

I declare I never heard or read of an army so partial to pastry as that British army before Sebastopol. I had a reputation for my sponge cakes that any pastry cook in London, even Gunter, might have been proud of. The officers, full of fun and high spirits, used to crowd into the little kitchen and, despite all my remonstrances (which were not always confined to words, for they made me frantic sometimes and an iron spoon is a tempting weapon), would carry the tarts hot from the oven, while the good-for-nothing black cooks, instead of lending me their aid, would stand by and laugh with all their teeth.

When the hot season commenced, the crowds that came to the British Hotel for my claret and cider cups and other cooling summer drinks, were very complimentary in their expressions of appreciation of my skill.

Now, supposing that you had made a hearty dinner and were thinking of starting homeward — if I can use so pleasant a term in reference to your cheerless quarters — it was very natural that you should be anxious to carry back something to your hut. Perhaps you expected to be sent into the trenches (many a supper cooked by me has been consumed in those fearful trenches by brave men who could eat it with keen appetites while the messengers of death were speeding around them), or perhaps you had planned a little dinner party and wanted to give your friends something better than their ordinary fare. Anyhow, you would in all probability have some good reason for returning laden with comforts and necessaries from Spring Hill. You would not even be very particular about carrying them yourself. You might have been a great swell at home, where you would have shuddered if Bond Street had seen you carrying a parcel no larger than your card case, but those considerations rarely troubled you here. Very likely, your servant was lying crouched in a rifle pit, taking 'pots' at the Russians, or keeping watch and ward in the long lines of trenches. Or, stripped to his shirt, shovelling powder and shot into the great guns, whose steady roar constantly broke the evening's calm. If you did not wait upon yourself, you would stand a very fair chance of being starved. So you would open your knapsack, if you had brought one, for me to fill it with potatoes and holler out, "Never mind, mother!" although the gravy from the fowls on your saddle before you, was soaking through the little modicum of paper which was all I could afford you. So laden, you would cheerfully start up the hill of mud hutward, and well for you if you did not come to grief on that treacherous sea of mud that lay swelling between the Col and your destination. Many a mishap, ludicrous but for their consequences, happened on it. I remember a young officer coming down one day just in time to carry off my last fowl and meat pie. Before he had gone far, the horse so floundered in the mud that the saddle girths broke and, while the pies rolled into the mud in one direction, the fowl flew in another. To make matters worse, the horse, in his efforts to extricate himself, did for them entirely and, in terrible distress, the poor fellow came back for me to set him up again. I shook my head for a long time, but at last, after he had over and over again urged upon me pathetically that he had two fellows coming to dine with him at six and nothing in the world in his hut but salt pork, I resigned a plump fowl which I had kept back for my own dinner. Off he started again, but soon came back with, "Oh, mother, I forgot all about the potatoes, they've all rolled out upon that road, you must fill my bag again."

We all laughed heartily at him, but this state of things had been rather tragic.

Before I bring this chapter to a close, I should like, with the reader's permission, to describe one day of my life in the Crimea. They were all pretty much alike, except when there was fighting upon a large scale going on and duty called me to the field.

I was generally up and busy by daybreak, sometimes earlier, for in the summer my bed had no attractions strong enough to bind me to it after four.

There was plenty to do before the work of the day began. There was the poultry to pluck and prepare for cooking, which had been killed on the previous night, the joints to be cut up and got ready for the same purpose, the medicines to be mixed, the store to be swept and cleaned. Of very great importance, with all these things to see after, were the few hours of quiet before the road came alive with travellers.

By seven o'clock, the morning coffee would be ready, hot and refreshing and eagerly sought for by the officers of the Army Works Corps engaged upon making the great high-road to the front, and the Commissariat and Land Transport men carrying stores from Balaclava to the heights. There was always a great demand for coffee by those who knew its refreshing and strengthening qualities. Milk I could not give them (I kept it in tins for special use), but the coffee was hot and strong, with plenty of sugar and a slice of butter, which I recommend as a capital substitute for milk. From that time until nine, officers on duty in the neighbourhood, or passing by, would look in for breakfast, and about half past nine my sick patients began to show themselves. In the following hour they would come thickly and sometimes it was past mid-day before I had got through this duty.

They came with every variety of suffering and disease. The cases I most disliked were the frostbitten fingers and feet in the winter.

That over, there was the hospital to visit across the way, which was sometimes overcrowded with patients.

I was a good deal there and, as often as possible, would take over books and papers, which I used to borrow for that purpose from my friends and the officers I knew. Once, a great packet of tracts was sent to me from Plymouth anonymously and these I distributed in the same manner.

By this time the day's news had come from the front and perhaps among the casualties overnight there would be someone wounded or sick, who would be glad to see me ride up with the comforts he stood most in need of and during the day, if any accident occurred in the neighbourhood or on the road near the British Hotel, the men generally brought the sufferer there, from where, if the hurt was serious, he would be transferred to the hospital of the Land Transport opposite. I used not always to stand upon too much ceremony when I heard of sick or wounded officers in the front. Sometimes their friends would ask me to go to them, though very often I waited for no hint, but took the chance of meeting with a kind reception. I used to think of their relatives at home, who would have given so much to possess my privilege. More than one officer have I startled by appearing before him and telling him abruptly that he must have a mother, wife, or sister at home whom he missed and that he must therefore be glad of some woman to take their place.

Until evening the store would be filled with customers waiting provisions, dinners and luncheons, loungers and idlers seeking conversation and amusement. At eight o'clock the curtain descended on that day's labour and I could sit down and eat at leisure. It was no easy thing to clear the store, canteen and yards, but we determined upon adhering to the rule that nothing should be sold after that hour, and succeeded. Anyone who came after that time, came simply as a friend. There could be no necessity for anyone, except on extraordinary occasions when the rule would be relaxed, to purchase things after eight o'clock.

Drunkenness or excess were discouraged at Spring Hill in every way. Indeed, my few unpleasant scenes arose chiefly from my refusing to sell liquor where I saw it was wanted to be abused. I could appeal with a clear conscience to all who knew me there, to back my assertion that I neither permitted drunkenness among the men, nor gambling among the officers. Whatever happened elsewhere, intoxication, cards and dice were never to be seen within the precincts of the British Hotel. My regulations were well known, and a kind-hearted officer of the Royals, who was much there and who permitted me to use a familiarity towards him which I trust I never abused, undertook to be my Provost Marshal, but his duties were very light.

At first we kept our store open on Sunday from sheer necessity, but after a little while, when stores in abundance were established at Kadikoi and elsewhere and the absolute necessity no longer existed, Sunday became a day of most grateful rest at Spring Hill. This step met with opposition from the men, but again we were determined and again we triumphed.

I am sure we needed rest. I have often wondered since how it was that I never fell ill or came home "on urgent private affairs." I am afraid that I was not sufficiently thankful to the Providence which gave me strength to carry out the work I loved so well and felt so happy in being engaged upon. Although I never had a week's illness during my campaign, the labour, anxiety and perhaps the few trials that followed it, have told upon me. I have never felt since that time, the strong and hearty woman that I was when I braved with impunity the pestilence of Navy Bay and Cruces.

It would kill me easily now.

CHAPTER 15

In the last three chapters, I have attempted, without any consideration of dates, to give my readers some idea of my life in the Crimea. I am fully aware that I have jumbled up events strangely, talking in the same page and even sentence, of events which occurred at different times, but I have three excuses to offer for my unhistorical inexactness In the first place, my memory is far from trustworthy and I kept no written diary. In the second place, the reader must have had more than enough of journals and chronicles of Crimean life and I am only the historian of Spring Hill. In the third place, unless I am allowed to tell the story of my life in my own way, I cannot tell it at all.

I shall now endeavour to describe my outdoor life as much as possible and write of those great events in the field of which I was a humble witness. But I shall continue to speak from my own experience simply and if the reader should be surprised at my leaving any memorable action of the army unnoticed, he may be sure that it is because I was missing medicines or making good things in the kitchen of the British Hotel and first heard the particulars of it, perhaps, from the newspapers which came from home. My readers must know, too, that they were much more familiar with the history of the camp at their own firesides, than we who lived in it. Just as a spectator seeing one of the battles from a hill, as I did the Tchernaya, knows more about it than the combatant in the valley below, who only thinks of the enemy whom it is his immediate duty to repel. So you, through the valuable aid of the cleverest man in the whole camp, read in the *Times* columns the details of that great campaign, while we, the actors in it, had enough to do to discharge our own duties well and rarely concerned ourselves with what seemed of such importance to you. And so very often a desperate skirmish or hard-fought action, the news of which created so much sensation in England, was but little regarded at Spring Hill.

My first experience of battle was pleasant enough. Before we had been long at Spring Hill, Omar Pasha got something for his Turks to do. One fine morning they were marched away towards the Russian outposts on the road to Baidar. I accompanied them on horseback and enjoyed the sight amazingly. English and French cavalry preceded the Turkish infantry over the plain, yet full of memories of the disastrous Light Cavalry charge a few months before. While one detachment of the Turks made a reconnaissance to the right of the Tchernaya, another pushed their way up the hill, towards Kamara, driving in the Russian outposts, after what seemed but a slight resistance. It was very pretty to see them advance, and to watch how every now and then little clouds of white smoke puffed up from behind bushes and the crests of hills and were answered by similar puffs from the long hue of busy skirmishers that preceded the main body.

This was my first experience of actual battle and I felt that strange excitement which I do not remember on future occasions, coupled with an earnest longing to see more of warfare and to share in its hazards. It was not long before my wish was gratified.

I do not know much of the second bombardment of

Sebastopol in the month of April, although I was as assiduous as I could be in my attendance at Cathcart's Hill. I could judge of its severity by the long trains of wounded which passed the British Hotel. I had a stretcher laid near the door and very often a poor fellow was laid upon it, outwearied by the terrible conveyance from the front.

After this unsuccessful bombardment, it seemed to us that there was a sudden lull in the progress of the siege and other things began to interest us. There were several arrivals to talk over. Miss Nightingale came to supervise the Balaclava hospitals and, before long, she had practical experience of Crimean fever. After her, came the Duke of Newcastle and the great high priest of the mysteries of cookery, Mons. Alexis Soyer. He was often at Spring Hill, with the most smiling of faces and in the most gorgeous of irregular uniforms and never failed to praise my soups and dainties. I always flattered myself that I was his match and with our West Indian dishes could of course beat him hollow. More than once I challenged him to a trial of skill, but the gallant Frenchman only shrugged his shoulders and disclaimed my challenge with many flourishes of his jewelled hands, declaring that Madame proposed a contest where victory would cost him his reputation for gallantry and be more disastrous than defeat.

All because I was a woman, forsooth. What nonsense to talk like that when I was doing the work of half a dozen men. Then he would laugh and declare that, when our campaigning were over, we would render rivalry impossible by combining to open the first restaurant in Europe. There was always fun in the store when the good-natured Frenchman was there.

One dark, tempestuous night, I was woken up by the

arrival of other guests. These were the first regiment of
Sardinian Grenadiers on their way to the position assigned
them. They remained at Spring Hill until the morning. We
soon turned out our staff and lighted up the store and
entertained the officers as well as we could inside while the
soldiers bivouacked in the yards around. Not a single thing
was stolen or disturbed that night, although they had many
opportunities. We all admired and liked the Sardinians.
They were honest, well-disciplined fellows and I wish there
had been no worse men or soldiers in the Crimea.

As the season advanced many visitors came to the
Crimea from all parts of the world and many of them were
glad to make Spring Hill their headquarters. We should
have been better off if some of them had spared us this
compliment. A Captain St. Clair, for instance — who could
doubt anyone with such a name? — stayed some time with
us, had the best of everything and paid us most honourably
with one bill upon his agents, while we cashed another to
provide him with money for his homeward route. He was
an accomplished fellow and I really liked him but,
unfortunately for us, he was a swindler.

I saw much of another visitor to the camp in the Crimea
— an old acquaintance of mine with whom I had had many
a hard bout in past times — the cholera. There were many
cases in the hospital of the Land Transport Corps opposite
and I prescribed for many others personally. The raki sold in
too many of the stores in Balaclava and Kadikoi was most
pernicious and although the authorities forbade the sutlers
to sell it, under heavy penalties, it found its way into the
camp in large quantities.

During May and while preparations were being made
for the third great bombardment of the ill-fated city, summer

broke beautifully and the weather, chequered occasionally by fitful intervals of cold and rain, made us all cheerful. You would scarcely have believed that the happy, good-humoured and jocular visitors to the British Hotel were the same men who had, a few weeks before, ridden gloomily through the muddy road to its door. It was a period of relaxation and they all enjoyed it.

Amusement was the order of the day. Races, doghunts, cricket matches and dinner parties were eagerly indulged in. Keen to provide the good cheer which was so essential a part of these entertainments when the warm weather came in all its intensity, I took to manufacturing cooling beverages for my friends and customers. My store was always full. To please all was somewhat difficult and occasionally some of them were scarcely so polite as they should have been to a perplexed hostess, who could scarcely be expected to remember that Lieutenant A. had ordered his sangaree an instant before Captain B. and his friends had ordered their claret cup.

In anticipation of the hot weather, I had laid in a large stock of raspberry vinegar which, properly managed, helps to make a pleasant drink. There was a great demand for sangaree, claret and cider cups (the cups being battered pewter pots).

Would you like, reader, to know my recipe for the favourite claret cup? It is simple enough. Claret, water, lemon peel, sugar, nutmeg and ice — yes, ice, but not often and not for long, for the eager officers soon finish it off.

Sometimes there were dinner parties at Spring Hill, but of these more hereafter. At one of the earliest, when the *Times* correspondent was to be present, I rode down to Kadikoi, bought some calico and cut it up into table napkins. They all laughed very heartily and thought perhaps of a few weeks previously, when every available piece of linen in the camp would have been snapped up for pocket handkerchiefs

But the reader must not forget that all this time, although there might be only a few short and sullen roars of the great guns by day, few nights passed without some fighting in the trenches and very often the news of the morning would be that one or other of those I knew had fallen. These tidings often saddened me and when I awoke in the night and heard the thunder of the guns fiercer than usual, I have quite dreaded the dawn which might usher in bad news.

The deaths in the trenches touched me deeply, perhaps for this reason. It was very usual, when a young officer was ordered into the trenches, for him to ride down to Spring Hill to dine, or obtain something more than his ordinary fare to brighten his weary hours in those fearful ditches. They seldom failed on these occasions to shake me by the hand at parting and sometimes would say:

"You see, Mrs. Seacole, I can't say goodbye to the dear ones at home, so I'll bid you goodbye for them. Perhaps you'll see them some day and if the Russians should knock me over, mother, just tell them I thought of them all — will you?"

Although all this might be said in a light-hearted manner, it was rather solemn. I felt it to be so, for I never failed (although who was I, that I should preach?) to say something about God's providence and relying upon it and they were very good. No army of parsons could be much better than my sons. They would listen very gravely and shake me by the hand again, while I felt that there was nothing in the world I would not do for them.

Then very often the men would say, "I'm going in with my master tonight, Mrs. Seacole, come and look after him, if he's hit."

So often as this happened I would pass the night restlessly, awaiting with anxiety the morning and yet dreading to hear the news it held in store for me. I used to think it was like having a large family of children ill with fever and dreading to hear which one had passed away in the night.

As often as the bad news came, I thought it my duty to ride up to the hut of the sufferer and do my woman's work. But I felt it deeply. How could it be otherwise? There was one poor boy in the Artillery, with blue eyes and light golden hair, whom I nursed through a long and weary sickness, borne with all a man's spirit, and whom I grew to love like a fond old fashioned mother. I thought if ever angels watched over any life, they would shelter his. Yet one day, but a short time after he had left his sickbed, he was struck down on his battery, working like a young hero.

It was a long time before I could banish from my mind the thought of him as I saw him last, the yellow hair, stiff and stained with his lifeblood and the blue eyes closed in the sleep of death. Of course, I saw him buried, as I did poor H.V., my old Jamaica friend, whose kind face was so familiar to me of old.

Captain B, of the Coldstreams was another good friend I mourned bitterly. He had been with me on the previous evening, had seemed dull, but had supped at my store and, on the following morning, a brother officer told me he was shot dead while setting his pickets, which made me ill and unfit for work for the whole day. Mind you, a day was a long time to give tomorrow in the Crimea.

I could give many other similar instances, but why should I sadden myself or my readers? Others have described the horrors of those fatal trenches, but their real history has never been written and perhaps it is as well that so harrowing a tale should be left in oblivion. Such anecdotes as the following were very current in the camp, but I have no means of answering for its truth.

Two sergeants met in the trenches, who had been schoolmates in their youth. Years had passed since they set out for the battle of life by different roads, and now they met again under the fire of a common enemy. With one impulse they started forward to exchange a hearty handshake and mutual greetings. While their hands were still clasped, a chance shot killed both.

CHAPTER 16

Before I left the Crimea to return to England, the Adjutant-General of the British Army gave me a testimonial, which the reader has already read, in which he stated that I had 'frequently exerted myself in the most praiseworthy manner in attending wounded men, even in positions of great danger'. The simple meaning of this sentence is that, in the discharge of what I conceived to be my duty, I was frequently under fire. Now I am far from wishing to speak of this fact with any vanity or pride. After all, one soon gets accustomed to it and it fails at last to create more than temporary uneasiness. Indeed, after Sebastopol was ours, you might often see officers strolling coolly, even leisurely, across and along those streets, exposed to the enemy's fire, when a little haste would have carried them beyond the reach of danger. The truth was, I believe, they had grown so habituated to being in peril from shot or shell, that they rather liked the sensation and found it difficult to get on without a little gratuitous excitement and danger.

But putting aside the great engagements where I underwent considerable peril, one could scarcely move about the various camps without some risk. The Russians had, it seemed, sunk great ships' guns into the earth, from which they fired shot and shell at a very long range, which came tumbling and plunging between and sometimes into the huts and tents, in a very unwieldy and generally harm-

less fashion. Once when I was riding through the camp of
the Rifles, a round shot came plunging towards me and
before I or the horse had time to be much frightened, the
ugly fellow buried itself in the earth, with a heavy thud, a
little distance in front of us.

In the first week of June, the third bombardment of
Sebastopol opened and the Spring Hill visitors had plenty to
talk about. Many were the surmises as to when the assault
would take place, of the success of which nobody
entertained a doubt. Somehow or other, important secrets
(which the Russians would have given much to know)
oozed out in various parts of the camp, and one of these
places was the British Hotel. Some such whispers were
afloat on the evening of Sunday the 17th of June, and excited
me strangely. Any stranger not in my secret would have
considered that my conduct fully justified my partner, Mr.
Day, in sending me home, as better fitted for a week in
bedlam than the charge of a hotel in the Crimea. I never
remember feeling more excited or more restless than upon
that day and no sooner had night fairly closed in upon us
than, instead of making preparations for bed, this same
stranger would have seen me wrap up — the nights were
very cold — and start off for a long walk to Cathcart's Hill,
three miles and a half away. I stayed there until past
midnight, but when I returned home, there was no rest for
me, for I had found out that, in the stillness of the night,
many regiments were marching down to the trenches and
that the dawn of day would be the signal that should let
them loose upon the Russians. The few hours still left before
daybreak were made the most of at Spring Hill. We were all
busily occupied in cutting bread and cheese and
sandwiches, packing up fowls, tongues and ham, wine and

spirits, while I carefully filled the large bag, which I always carried into the field slung across my shoulder, with lint, bandages, needles, thread and medicines. Soon after daybreak everything was ready packed upon two mules in the charge of my steadiest lad and, I leading the way on horseback, the little cavalcade left the British Hotel before the sun of the fatal 18th of June had been many hours old.

It was not long before our progress was arrested by the cavalry pickets closely stationed to stop all stragglers and spectators from reaching the scene of action. But after a slight parley and when they found out who I was and how I was prepared for the day's work, the men raised a shout for me and, with their officer's sanction, allowed me to pass.

So I reached Cathcart's Hill crowded with non-combatants and, leaving there the mules, loaded myself with what provisions I could carry and — it was a work of no little difficulty and danger — succeeded in reaching the reserves of Sir Henry Barnard's division, which was to have stormed something, I forget what, but when they found the attack upon the Redan was a failure, very wisely abstained. Here I found plenty of officers who soon relieved me of my refreshments and some wounded men who found the contents of my bag very useful. At length I made my way to the Woronzoff Road, where the temporary hospital had been erected. There I found the doctors hard enough at work and hastened to help them as best I could. I bound up the wounds and ministered to the wants of a good many, staying there some considerable time.

Upon the way and even here, I was under fire. More frequently than was agreeable. A shot would come ploughing up the ground and raising clouds of dust, or a shell whizz above us. Upon these occasions those around would cry out, "Lie down, mother, lie down!" and with very undignified and unladylike haste I had to embrace the earth and remain there until the same voices would laughingly assure me that the danger was over, or one, more thoughtful than the rest, would come to give me a helping hand and hope that the old lady was neither hit nor frightened.

Several times in my wanderings on that eventful day (of which I confess to have a most confused remembrance, only knowing that I looked after many wounded men), I was ordered back, but each time my bag of bandages and comforts for the wounded proved my passport.

While at the hospital I was chiefly of use looking after those who, either from lack of hands or because their hurts were less serious, had to wait, pained and weary, until the kind-hearted doctors — who, however, looked more like murderers — could attend to them. And the grateful words and smile which rewarded me for binding up a wound or giving cooling drink was a pleasure worth risking life for at any time.

It was here that I received my only wound during the campaign. I threw myself too hastily on the ground, in obedience to the command of those around me, to escape a threatening shell and fell heavily on the thumb of my right hand, dislocating it.

It was bound up on the spot and did not inconvenience me much, but it has never returned to its proper shape.

After this, first washing my hands in some sherry from lack of water, I went back to Cathcart's Hill, where I found my horse and heard that the good-for-nothing lad, either frightened or tired of waiting, had gone away with the mules. I had to ride three miles after him and then the only satisfaction I had arose from laying my horsewhip about his shoulders.

After that, working my way round, how I can scarcely tell, I got to the extreme left attack, where General Eyre's division had been hotly engaged all day and had suffered severely. I left my horse in charge of some men and, with no little difficulty and at no little risk, crept down to where some wounded men lay, with whom I left refreshments. And then — it was grow ing late — I started for Spring Hill, where I heard all about the events of the luckless day from those who had seen them from posts of safety, while I, who had been in the midst of it all day, knew so little.

On the following day some Irishmen of the 8th Royals brought me, in token of my having been among them, a Russian woman's dress and a poor pigeon, which they had brought away from one of the houses in the suburb where their regiment suffered so severely.

But that evening of the 18th of June was a sad one and the news that came in of those that had fallen was most heart-rending. Both the leaders, who fell so gloriously before the Redan, had been very good to the mistress of Spring Hill. But a few days before the 18th, Col. Y. had merrily declared that I should have a silver salver to hand about things upon, instead of the poor shabby one I had been reduced to, while Sir John C. had been my kind patron for some years. It was in my house in Jamaica that Lady C. had once lodged when her husband was stationed in that island. And when the recall home came, Lady C., who, had she been like most women, would have shrunk from any assertion, declared that she was a soldier's wife and would accompany him. Fortunately the *Blenheim* was detained in the roads a few days after the time expected for her departure and I put into its father's arms a little Scotchman, born within sight of the blue hills of Jamaica. And yet with these at home, the brave general — as I read in the *Times* a few weeks later — displayed a courage amounting to rashness and, sending away his aides-de-camp, rushed on to a certain death.

On the following day, directly I heard of the armistice, I hastened to the scene of action, anxious to see once more the faces of those who had been so kind to me in life. That battlefield was a fearful sight for a woman to witness, and if I do not pray God that I may never see its like again, it is because I wish to be useful all my life and it is in scenes of horror and distress that a woman can do so much, It was late in the afternoon, about half-past four, that the Russians brought over the bodies of the two leaders of yesterday's assault. They had stripped Sir John of epaulettes, sword and boots.

How my heart felt for those at home who would so soon hear of this day's fatal work.

It was on the following day, I think, that I saw them bury him near Cathcart's Hill, where his tent had been pitched. If I had been in the least humour for what was ludicrous, the looks and curiosity of the Russians who saw me during the armistice would have afforded me considerable amusement. I wonder what rank they assigned me.

How true it is, as somebody has said, that misfortunes never come singly. N.B. Pleasures often do. For while we were dull enough at this great trouble, we had cholera raging around us, carrying off its victims of all ranks.

There was great distress in the Sardinian camp on this account and I soon lost another good customer, General E., carried off by the same terrible plague.

Before Mrs. E. left the Crimea, she sent several useful

things, kept back from the sale of the general's effects. At this sale I wanted to buy a useful wagon, but did not like to bid against Lord W., who purchased it, but (I tell this anecdote to show how kind they all were to me) when his lordship heard of this he sent it over to Spring Hill, with a message that it was mine for a far lower price than he had given for it. Since my return home I have had to thank the same nobleman for still greater favours.

But who, indeed, has not been kind to me?

Within a week after General E's death, a still greater calamity happened. Lord Raglan died — that great soldier who had such iron courage, with the gentle smile and kind words that always show the good man. I was familiar enough with his person, for, although people did not know it in England, he was continually in the saddle looking after his suffering men and scheming plans for their benefit. And the humblest soldier will remember that, let who might look stern and distant, the first man in the British army ever had a kind word to give him.

During the time he was ill I was at headquarters several times and once his servants allowed me to peep into the room where their master lay. I do not think they knew that he was dying, but they seemed very sad and low — far more so than he for whom they feared. On the day of his funeral I was there again. I never saw such heartfelt gloom as that which brooded on the faces of his attendants, but it was good to hear how they all, even the humblest, had some kind memory of the great general whom Providence had called from his post at such a season of danger and distress. Once again they let me into the room in which the coffin lay and I timidly stretched out my hand and touched a corner of the Union Jack which lay upon it and then I watched it wind

its way through the long lines of soldiery towards
Kamierch, while, ever and anon, the guns thundered forth
in sorrow, not in anger. And for days after I could not help
thinking of the *Caradoc*, which was ploughing its way
through the sunny sea with its sad burden.

It was not in the nature of the British army to remain long
dull and before very long we went on gaily as ever,
forgetting the terrible 18th of June, or only remembering it
to look forward to the next assault compensating for all.
And once more the British Hotel was filled with a busy
throng, laughter and fun echoed through its iron rafters.
Nothing of consequence was done in the front for weeks,
possibly because Mr. Russell was taking holiday and would
not return until August.

About this time the stores of the British Hotel were well
filled, not only with every conceivable necessary of life, but
with many of its most expensive luxuries. It was at this
period that you could have asked for few things that I could
not have supplied you with on the spot, or obtained for you,
if you had a little patience and did not mind a few weeks'
delay. Not only Spring Hill and Kadikoi, which — a poor
place enough when we came — had grown into a town of
stores and had its market regulations and police, but the
whole camp shared in this unusual plenty. Even the men
could afford to despise salt meat and pork and fed as well,
if not better, than if they had been in quarters at home. And
there were coffee houses and places of amusement opened
at Balaclava and balls given in some of them, which raised
my temper to an unwanted pitch, because I foresaw the
daggers which they had for the young and impulsive and
sure enough they cost several officers their commissions.

Right glad was I one day when the great purifier, Fire,

burnt down the worst of these places and ruined its owner, a bad French woman. And the railway was in full work and the great road nearly finished and the old one passable and the mules and horses looked in such fair condition, that you would scarcely have believed Farrier C., of the Land Transport Corps, who would have told you then and will tell you now, that he superintended, on one bleak morning of February, not six months ago, the task of throwing the corpses of one hundred and eight mules over the cliffs at Karanyi into the Black Sea beneath.

Of course the summer introduced its own plagues and among the worst of these were the flies. I shall never forget those Crimean flies and most sincerely hope that, like the Patagonians, they are only to be found in one part of the world. Nature must surely have intended them for black beetles and accidentally given them wings. There was no exterminating them, no escaping from them by night or by day. One of my boys confined himself almost entirely to laying baits and traps for their destruction and used to boast that he destroyed them at the rate of a gallon a day, but I never noticed any perceptible decrease in their powers of mischief and annoyance. The officers in the front suffered terribly from them. One of my kindest customers, a lieutenant serving in the Royal Naval Brigade, who was a close relative of the Queen, whose uniform he wore, came to me in great perplexity. He evidently considered the fly nuisance the most trying portion of the campaign and of far more consequence than the Russian shot and shell.

"Mammy," he said (he had been in the West Indies and so called me by the familiar term used by the Creole children), "Mammy, these flies respect nothing. Not content with eating my prog, they set to at night and make a supper of me." His face showed traces of the attacks. "Confound them, they'll kill me, mammy, they're everywhere, even in the trenches and you'd suppose they wouldn't care to go there from choice. What can you do for me, mammy?"

Not much, but I rode down to Mr. B.'s store, at Kadikoi, where I was lucky in being able to procure a piece of muslin, which I pinned up (time was too precious to allow me to use needle and thread) into a mosquito net, with which the prince was delighted. He fell ill later in the summer, when I went up to his quarters and did all I could for him.

As the summer wore on, busily passed by all of us at the British Hotel, rumours stronger than ever were heard of a great battle soon to be fought by the reinforcements which were known to have joined the Russian army.

I think that no one was much surprised when, at early dawn one pleasant August morning, heavy firing was heard towards the French position on the right, by the Tchernaya and the stream of troops and onlookers poured from all quarters in that direction. Prepared and loaded as usual, I was soon riding in the same direction and saw the chief part of the morning's battle. I saw the Russians cross and recross the river. I saw their officers cheer and wave them on in the coolest, bravest manner, until they were shot down by scores. I was near enough to hear at times, in the lull of artillery and above the rattle of the musketry, the excited cheers which told of a daring attack or a successful repulse and beneath where I stood I could see what the Russians could not — steadily drawn up, quiet and expectant, the squadrons of English and French cavalry, calmly yet impatiently waiting until the Russians' partial success should bring their sabres into play.

But the contingency never happened and we saw the

Russians fall slowly back in good order, while the dark plumed Sardinians and red-pantalooned French spread out in pursuit and formed a picture so excitingly beautiful that we forgot the suffering and death they left behind. And then I descended with the rest into the field of battle.

It was a fearful scene, but why repeat this remark. All death is trying to witness — even that of the good man who lays down his life hopefully and peacefully. On the battlefield, when the poor body is torn and rent in hideous ways and the scared spirit struggles to loose itself from the still strong frame that holds it tightly to the last, death is fearful indeed. It had come peacefully enough to some. They lay with half-opened eyes and a quiet smile about the lips that showed their end to have been painless, others it had arrested in the heat of passion and frozen on their pallid faces a glare of hatred and defiance that made your warm blood run cold. But little time had we to think of the dead, whose business it was to see after the dying who might yet be saved. The ground was thickly covered with the wounded, some of them calm and resigned, others impatient and restless, a few filling the air with their cries of pain — all wanting water and grateful to those who administered it and more substantial comforts. You might see officers and strangers, visitors to the camp, riding about the field on this errand of mercy. And this, although — surely it could not have been intentional — Russian guns still played upon the scene of action.

There were many others there, bent on a more selfish task. The plunderers were busy everywhere. It was marvellous to see how eagerly the French stripped the dead of what was valuable, not always paying much regard to the presence of a lady. Some of the officers, when I complained rather angrily, laughed and said it was spoiling the Egyptians, but I do think the Israelites spared their enemies those garments which, perhaps, were not so unmentionable in those days as they have since become.

I attended to the wounds of many French and Sardinians and helped to lift them into the ambulances, which came tearing up to the scene of action. I derived no little gratification from being able to dress the wounds of several Russians, indeed, they were as kindly treated as the others. One of them was badly shot in the lower jaw and was beyond my or any human skill. Incautiously I inserted my finger into his mouth to feel where the ball had lodged and his teeth closed upon it, in the agonies of death, so tightly that I had to call to those around to release it which was not done until it had been bitten so deeply that I shall carry the scar with me to my grave. Poor fellow, he meant me no harm, for as the near approach of death softened his features, a smile spread over his rough inexpressive face and so he died.

I attended another Russian, a handsome fellow and an officer, shot in the side, who bore his cruel suffering with a firmness that was very noble. In return for the little use I was to him, he took a ring off his finger and gave it to me. After I had helped to lift him into the ambulance he kissed my hand and smiled far more thanks than I had earned. I do not know whether he survived his wounds, but I fear not. Many others, on that day, gave me thanks in words the meaning of which was lost upon me and all of them in that one common language of the whole world — smiles.

I carried two patients off the field, one a French officer wounded on the hip, who chose to go back to Spring Hill and be attended by me there and who, on leaving, told us that he was a relative of the Marshal (Pelissier); the other, a poor Cossack colt I found running round its dam, which lay beside its Cossack master dead, with its tongue hanging from its mouth. The colt was already wounded in the ears and fore-foot and I was only just in time to prevent a French corporal who, perhaps for pity's sake, was preparing to give it it's *coup de grace*. I saved the poor thing by promising to give the Frenchman ten shillings if he would bring it down to the British Hotel, which he did that same evening. I attended to its hurts and succeeded in rearing it, and it became a great pet at Spring Hill and accompanied me to England.

I picked up some trophies from the battlefield, but not many, and those of little value. I cannot bear the idea of plundering either the living or the dead, but I picked up a Russian metal cross and took from the bodies of some of the poor fellows nothing of more value than a few buttons, which I severed from their coarse grey coats.

So end my reminiscences of the battle of the Tchernaya, fought, as all the world knows, on the 16th of August, 1855.

CHAPTER 17

The three weeks following the battle of the Tchernaya were, I should think, some of the busiest and most eventful the world has ever seen. There was little doing at Spring Hill. Every one was either at his post, or too anxiously awaiting the issue of the last great bombardment to spend much time at the British Hotel. I think that I lost more of my patients and customers during those few weeks than during the whole previous progress of the siege. Scarcely a night passed that I was not lulled to sleep with the heavy continuous roar of the artillery, scarce a morning dawned that the same sound did not usher in my day's work. The ear grew so accustomed during those weeks to the terrible roar, that when Sebastopol fell the sudden quiet seemed unnatural and made us dull.

During the whole of this time the most perplexing rumours flew about, some having reference to the day of assault, the majority relative to the last great effort which it was supposed the Russians would make to drive us into the sea. I confess these latter rumours now and then caused me temporary uneasiness, Spring Hill being on the direct line of route which the actors in such a tragedy must take.

I spent much of my time on Cathcart's Hill, watching with a curiosity and excitement which became intense, the progress of the terrible bombardment. Now and then a shell would fall among the crowd of onlookers which covered the hill, but it never disturbed us, so keen and feverish and so deadened to danger had the excitement and expectation made us.

In the midst of the bombardment took place the important ceremony of distributing the Order of the Bath to those selected for that honour. I contrived to witness this ceremony very pleasantly and, although it cost me a day, I considered that I had fairly earned the pleasure. I was anxious to have some personal share in the affair, so I made and forwarded to headquarters, a cake which Gunter might have been at some loss to manufacture with the materials at my command and which I adorned gaily with banners, flags, etc. I received great kindness from the officials at the ceremony and from the officers — some of rank — who recognised me, indeed, I held quite a little *levée* around my chair.

Well, a few days after this ceremony, I thought the end of the world, instead of the war, was at hand, when every battery opened and poured a perfect hail of shot and shell upon the beautiful city which I had left the night before sleeping so calm and peaceful beneath the stars. The firing began at early dawn and was fearful. Sleep was impossible, so I arose and set out for my old station on Cathcart's Hill. And here, with refreshments for the anxious onlookers, I spent most of my time, right glad of any excuse to witness the last scene of the siege. It was from this spot that I saw fire after fire break out in Sebastopol and watched all night the beautiful yet terrible effect of a great ship blazing in the harbour and lighting up the adjoining country for miles.

The weather changed, as it often did in the Crimea, most capriciously and the morning of the memorable 8th of September broke cold and wintry. The same little bird which had let me into so many secrets, also gave me a hint of what this day was pregnant with and very early in the morning I was on horseback, with my bandages and refreshments ready to repeat the work of the 18th of June last. A line of sentries forbade all strangers passing through without orders, even to Cathcart's Hill, but once more I found that my reputation served as a permit and the officers relaxed the rule in my favour everywhere. So, early in the day, I was in my old spot, with my old appliances for the wounded and fatigued, little expecting however, that this day would so closely resemble the day of the last attack in its disastrous results.

It was noon before the cannonading suddenly ceased and we saw, with a strange feeling of excitement, the French tumble out of their advanced trenches and roll into the Malakhoff like a human flood. Onward they seemed to go into the dust and smoke, swallowed up by hundreds, but they never returned and before long we saw workmen levelling parapets and filling up ditches, over which they drove with headlong speed and impetuosity, artillery and ammunition wagons, until there could be no doubt that the Malakhoff was taken, although the tide of battle still surged around it with violence and wounded men being borne from it in large numbers. Before this, our men had made their attack and the fearful assault of the Redan was going on and failing. But I was soon too busy to see much, for the wounded were brought to me in even greater numbers than at the last assault, whilst stragglers, slightly hurt, limped in, in fast-increasing numbers and engrossed our attention. I now and then found time to ask them rapid questions, but they did not appear to know anything more than that everything had gone wrong. The sailors, as before, showed their gallantry and even recklessness, conspicuously. The wounded of the ladder and sandbag parties came up even with a laugh and joked about their hurts in the happiest possible manner.

I saw many officers of the 97th wounded and, as far as possible, I reserved my attentions for my old regiment, known so well in my native island.

My poor 97th, their loss was terrible. I dressed the wound of one of its officers, seriously hit in the mouth. I attended to another wounded in the throat and bandaged the hand of a third, terribly crushed by a rifle bullet. In the midst of this we were often interrupted by those unwelcome and impartial Russian visitors — the shells. One fell so near that I thought my last hour was come and, although I had sufficient firmness to throw myself upon the ground, I was so seriously frightened that I never thought of rising from my recumbent position until the hearty laugh of those around convinced me that the danger had passed by. Afterwards I picked up a piece of this huge shell and brought it home with me.

It was on this, as on every similar occasion, that I saw the *Times* correspondent eagerly taking down notes and sketches of the scene, under fire — listening apparently with attention to all the busy little crowd that surrounded him, but without laying down his pencil and yet finding time, even in his busiest moment, to lend a helping hand to the wounded. It may have been on this occasion that his keen eye noticed me and his mind, albeit engrossed with far more important memories, found room to remember me. I may well be proud of his testimony, borne so generously only the other day and may well be excused for transcribing it from the columns of the *Times*:

*I have seen her go down, under fire, with her little store of
creature comforts for our wounded men and a more tender or
skillful hand about a wound or broken limb could not be found
among our best surgeons. I saw her at the assault on the Redan, at
the Tchernaya, at the fall of Sebastopol, laden, not with plunder
(good old soul), but with wine, bandages and food for the wounded
or the prisoners.*

I remained on Cathcart's Hill far into the night and watched
the city blazing beneath us, awestruck at the terrible sight,
until the bitter wind found its way through my thin clothing
and chilled me to the bone. Not till then did I leave.

I had little sleep. The night was made a ruddy lurid day
with the glare of the blazing town, while every now and
then came reports which shook the earth to its centre. And
yet I believe very many of the soldiers, wearied with their
day's labour, slept soundly throughout that terrible night
and awoke to find their work completed. For in the night,
covered by the burning city, Sebastopol was left, a heap of
ruins, to its victors and before noon on the following day,
none but dead and dying Russians were in the south side of
the once famous and beautiful mistress-city of the Euxine.

The good news soon spread through the camp. It gave
great pleasure, but I almost think the soldiers would have
been better pleased had the Russians delayed their parting
twelve hours longer and given the Highlanders a chance of
retrieving the disasters of the previous day. Nothing else
could wipe away the soreness of defeat, or compensate for
the better fortune which had befallen our allies the French.

The news of the evacuation of Sebastopol soon carried
away all traces of yesterday's fatigue. For weeks past I had

been offering bets to every one that I would not only be the first woman to enter Sebastopol from the English lines, but that I would be the first to carry refreshments into the fallen city. And now the time I had longed for had come. I borrowed some mules from the Land Transport Corps — mine were knocked up by yesterday's work — and loading them with good things, started off with my partner and some other friends early on that memorable Sunday morning for Cathcart's Hill.

When I found that strict orders had been given to admit no one inside Sebastopol, I became quite excited and making my way to General Garrett's quarters, I made such an earnest representation of what I considered my right that I soon obtained a pass, of which the following is a copy:

Pass Mrs. Seacole and her attendants, with refreshments for officers and soldiers in the Redan and in Sebastopol.
Cathcart's Hill Sept. 9,1855
GARRETT, M. G.

So many attached themselves to my staff, becoming for the nonce my attendants, that I had some difficulty at starting, but at last I passed all the sentries safely, much to the annoyance of many officers, who were trying every conceivable scheme to evade them, and entered the city.

I can give you no very clear description of its condition on that Sunday morning, a year and a half ago. Many parts of it were still blazing furiously — explosions were taking place in all directions — every step had a score of dangers and yet curiosity and excitement carried us on and on. I was often stopped to give refreshments to officers and men, who had been fasting for hours. Some, on the other hand, had found their way to Russian cellars and one body of men were most ingloriously drunk and playing the wildest pranks. They were dancing, yelling and singing — some of them with Russian women's dresses fastened round their waists and old bonnets stuck upon their heads.

I was offered many trophies. All plunder was stopped by the sentries and confiscated, so that the soldiers could afford to be liberal. By one I was offered a great velvet sofa, another pressed upon me a huge armchair, which had graced some Sebastopol study, while a third begged my acceptance of a portion of a grand piano. What I did carry away was very unimportant — a gaily-decorated altar candle, studded with gold and silver stars, which the present Commander-in-Chief condescended to accept as a Sebastopol memorial, an old cracked China teapot, which in happier times had very likely dispensed pleasure to many a small tea party, a cracked bell, which had rung many to prayers during the siege and which I bore away on my saddle, and a parasol, given me by a drunken soldier. He had a silk skirt on and torn lace upon his wrists and he came mincingly up, holding the parasol above his head and imitating the walk of an affected lady, to the vociferous delight of his comrades. And all this and much more, in that fearful charnel city, with death and suffering on every side.

It was very hazardous to pass along some of the streets exposed to the fire of the Russians on the north side of the harbour. We had to wait and watch our opportunity and then gallop for it. Some of us had close shaves of being hit. More than this, fires still kept breaking out around, while mines and fougasses not unfrequently exploded from unknown causes. We saw two officers emerge from a heap of ruins, covered and almost blinded with smoke and dust, from some such explosion. With considerable difficulty we succeeded in getting into the quarter of the town held by the French, where I was nearly getting into serious trouble.

I had loitered somewhat behind my party, watching, with pardonable curiosity, the adroitness with which a party of French were plundering a house. By the time my curiosity had been satisfied, I found myself quite alone, my retinue having preceded me by some few hundred yards. This would have been of little consequence had not an American sailor lad, actuated either by mischief or folly, whispered to the Frenchmen that I was a Russian spy and had they not, instead of laughing at him, credited his assertion and proceeded to arrest me. Now, such a charge was enough to make a lion of a lamb, so I refused positively to dismount and made matters worse by knocking in the cap of the first soldier who laid hands upon me with the bell that hung at my saddle. Upon this, six or seven tried to force me to the guardhouse in rather a rough manner. I resisted with all my force, screaming out for Mr. Day and using the bell for a weapon. How I longed for a better one, I need not tell the reader. In the midst of this scene came a French officer, whom I recognised as the patient I had taken to Spring Hill after the battle of the Tchernaya. He took my part at once and ordered them to release me.

Although it weakened my cause it was natural that, directly I was released, I should fly at the varlet who caused me this trouble. I did so, using my bell most effectually aided, when my party returned, by their riding whips.

This little adventure took up altogether so much time that, when the French soldiers had made their apologies to me and I had returned the compliment to the one whose head had been dented by my bell, it was growing late and we made our way back to Cathcart's Hill.

On the way, a French soldier begged me to buy a picture, which had been cut from above the altar of a church in Sebastopol. I ultimately became its possessor and brought it home with me. It is some eight or ten feet in length and represents, I should think, the Madonna. I am no judge of such things, but I think, although the painting is rather coarse, that the face of the Virgin and the heads of Cherubim that fill the cloud from which she is descending, are soft and beautiful. There is a look of divine calmness and heavenly love in the Madonna's face which is very striking and, perhaps, during the long and awful siege many a knee was bent in worship before it and many a heart found comfort in its soft, loving gaze.

On the following day I again entered Sebastopol and saw still more of its horrors. But I have refrained from describing so many scenes of woe, that I am loathe to dwell much on these. The very recollection of that woeful hospital where thousands of dead and dying had been left by the retreating Russians, is enough to unnerve the strongest and sicken the most experienced. I would give much if I had never seen that harrowing sight. I believe some Englishmen were found in it alive, but it was as well that they did not live to tell their fearful experience.

I went into the Redan also, although every step was dangerous, took from it some brown bread, which seemed to have been left in the oven by the baker when he died.

Before long, some Frenchwomen opened houses in Sebastopol, but in that quarter of the town held by the English the prospect was not sufficiently tempting for me to follow their example and so I saw out the remainder of the campaign from my old quarters at Spring Hill.

CHAPTER 18

Well, the great work was accomplished — Sebastopol was taken. The Russians had retired sullenly to their stronghold on the north side of the harbour, from which, every now and then, they sent a few vain shot and shell, which sent the amateurs in the streets of Sebastopol scampering, but gave the experienced no concern. In a few days the camp could find plenty to talk about in their novel position — and what then? What was to be done? More fighting? Another equally terrible and lengthy siege of the north? That was the business of a few at headquarters and in Council at home, between whom the electric wires flashed many a message. In the meanwhile, the real workers applied themselves to plan amusements and the same energy and activity which had made Sebastopol a heap of ruins and a well-filled cemetery; which had dug the miles of trenches and held them when made against a desperate foe; which had manned the many guns and worked them so well, set to work as eager to kill their present enemy, Time, as they had lately been to destroy their fled enemies, the Russians.

All who were before Sebastopol will long remember the beautiful autumn which succeeded to so eventful a summer and ushered in so pleasantly the second winter of the campaign. It was appreciated as only those who earn the right to enjoyment can enjoy relaxation. The camp was full of visitors of every rank. They thronged the streets of

Sebastopol, sketching its ruins and setting up photographic apparatus in contemptuous indifference of the shot with which the Russians generally favoured every conspicuous group.

Pleasure was hunted keenly. Cricket matches, picnics, dinner parties, races, theatricals — all found their admirers.

My restaurant was always full and once more merry laughter was heard and many a dinner party was held beneath the iron roof of the British Hotel. Several were given in compliment to our allies and many distinguished Frenchmen have tested my powers of cooking. You might have seen at one party some of their most famous officers.

At once were present a Prince of the Imperial family of France, the Duc de Rouchefoucault and a certain corporal in the French service, who was perhaps the best known man in the whole army, the Viscount Talon. They expressed themselves highly gratified at the food and perhaps were not a little surprised as course after course made its appearance. Soup and fish succeeded turkeys, saddle of mutton, fowls, ham, tongue, curry, pastry of many sorts, custards, jelly, blancmange and olives. I took a peculiar pride in doing my best when they were present, for I knew a little of the secrets of the French commissariat. I wonder if the world will ever know more. I wonder if the system of secrecy which has so long kept veiled the sufferings of the French army before Sebastopol will ever yield to truth. I used to guess something of those sufferings when I saw, even after the fall of Sebastopol, half-starved French soldiers prowling about my store, taking eagerly even what the Turks rejected as unfit for human food. No one could accuse them of squeamishness. I cannot but believe that in some desks or bureaux lie notes or diaries which shall one day be given to the world and when this happens, the terrible distresses of the English army will pall before the unheardof sufferings of the French. It is true that they carried from Sebastopol the lion's share of glory. My belief is that they deserved it, having borne by far a larger proportion of suffering.

There were few dinners at Spring Hill at which the guests did not show their appreciation of their hostess's labour by drinking her health. At the one I have alluded to, the toast was responded to with such enthusiasm that I felt compelled to put my acknowledgments into the form of a little speech, which Talon interpreted to his countrymen.

The French Prince was, after this occasion, several times at the British Hotel. He was there once when some Americans were received by me with scarcely that cordiality which I have been told distinguished my reception of guests and upon their leaving I told him — quite forgetting his own connection with America — of my prejudice against the Yankees. He heard me for a little while and then he interrupted me.

"*Tenez!* Madame Seacole, I too am American a little."

What a pity I was not born a countess, I am sure I should have made a great courtier. Witness my impromptu answer:

"I should never have guessed it, Prince."

He seemed amused.

With the theatricals directly I had nothing to do. Had I been a little younger the companies would very likely have been glad of me, for no one liked to sacrifice their beards to become Miss Julia or plain Mary Ann. Even the beardless subalterns had voices which no coaxing could soften down. But I lent them plenty of dresses, indeed, it was the only airing which a great many gay-coloured muslins had in the

Crimea. How was I to know when I brought them what camplife was? In addition to this, I found it necessary to convert my kitchen into a temporary green room where, to the wonderment and perhaps scandal of the black cook, the ladies of the company of the 1st Royals were taught to manage their petticoats with becoming grace and neither to show their awkward booted ankles, nor trip themselves up over their trains. It was a difficult task in many respects. Although I laced them in until they grew blue in the face, their waists were a disgrace to the sex, while my struggles to give them becoming *embonpoint* may be imagined. It was not until a year later that *Punch* thought of using a clothes basket. I would have given much for such a hint when I was dresser to the theatrical company of the 1st Royals.

The hair was another difficulty. To be sure, there was plenty in the camp, only it was in the wrong place and many an application was made to me for a set of curls. However, I am happy to say I have not become a customer of the wigmakers yet.

My recollections of hunting in the Crimea are confined to seeing troops of horsemen sweep by with shouts and yells after some wretched dog. Once I was very nearly frightened out of my wits — my first impression being that the Russians had carried into effect their old threat of driving us into the sea — by the startling appearance of a large body of horsemen tearing down the hill after, apparently, nothing. I discovered in good time that, in default of vermin, they were chasing a brother officer with a paper bag.

My experience of Crimean races are perfect, for I was present, in the character of cantiniere, at all the more important meetings. Some of them took place before Christmas and some after, but I shall exhaust the subject at

once. I had no little difficulty to get the things on to the
course and in particular, after I had sat up the whole night
making preparations for the December races, at the
monastery of St. George, I could not get my poor mules over
the rough country and found myself, in the middle of the
day, some miles from the course. I finally gave it up as
hopeless and, dismounting, sat down by the roadside to
consider how I could possibly dispose of the piles of
sandwiches, bread, cheese, pies and tarts which had been
prepared for the hungry spectators. Eventually, some
officers, who expected me long before, came to look for me
and with their assistance we reached the course.

I was better off at the next meeting, for a kind-hearted
Major of Artillery provided me with a small bell-tent that
enabled me to keep my stores out of reach of the light-
fingered gentry, who were as busy in the Crimea as at
Epsom or Hampton Court. Over this tent waved the flag of
the British Hotel, but during the day, it was used for an
accident happening to one Captain D. He was brought to
my tent insensible, where I quickly improvised a couch of
some straw, covered with the Union Jack and brought him
round. I mention this trifle to show how ready of
contrivance a little campaigning causes one to become.

I had several patients in consequence of accidents at the
races. Nor was I altogether free from accidents myself. On
the occasion of the races by the Tchemaya, after the
armistice, my cart, on turning a sudden bend in the steep
track, rolled over. Its contents of plates and dishes were
completely broken, so that I was reduced to hand out
sandwiches on broken pieces of earthenware and scraps of
paper. I saved some glasses, but not many and some of the

officers were obliged to drink out of stiff paper twisted into funnel-shaped glasses.

It was astonishing how well the managers of these Crimean races had contrived to imitate the old familiar scenes at home. You might well wonder where the racing saddles and boots and silk caps and jackets had come from, but our connection with England was very different to what it had been when I first came to the Crimea and many a wife and sister's fingers had been busy making the racing gear for the Crimea meetings. And in order that the course should still more closely resemble Ascot or Epsom, some soldiers blackened their faces and came out as Ethiopian serenaders, although it would puzzle the most ingenious to guess where they got their wigs and banjoes from. I caught one of them behind my tent in the act of knocking off the neck of a bottle of champagne and, paralysed by the wine's hasty exit, the only excuse he offered was that he wanted to know if the officers' luxury was better than rum.

A few weeks before Christmas, happened that fearful explosion in the French ammunition park, which destroyed so many lives. We had experienced nothing at all like it before. The earth beneath us, even at the distance of three miles, reeled and trembled with the shock. So great was the force of the explosion, that a piece of stone was hurled with some violence against the door of the British Hotel.

We all felt for the French very much, although I do not think that the armies agreed quite so well after the taking of the Malakhoff and the unsuccessful assault upon the Redan, as they had done previously. I saw several instances of unpleasantness and collision arising from allusions to sore points. One, in particular occurred in my store.

The French, when they wanted — it was very seldom —

to wound the pride of the English soldiery, used to say significantly in that jargon by which the various nations in the Crimea endeavoured to obviate the consequences of what occurred at the Tower of Babel, some time ago, "Malakhoff bono — Redan no bono."

This, of course, usually led to recriminatory statements and history was ransacked to find something consolatory to English pride. Once I noticed a brawny man, of the Army Works Corps bringing a small French Zouave to my canteen, evidently with the view of treating him. The Frenchman seemed mischievously inclined and, probably relying upon the good humour on the countenance of his gigantic companion, began a little playful bantering, ending with the taunt of "Redan, no bono! Redan, no bono!"

I never saw any man look so helplessly angry as the Englishman did. For a few minutes he seemed absolutely rooted to the ground.

He could have crushed his mocking friend with ease, but how could he answer his taunt. All at once, however, a happy thought struck him and rushing up to the Zouave, he caught him round the waist and threw him down, roaring out, "Waterloo was bono! Waterloo was bono!"

It was as much as the people on the premises could do to part them, so convulsed were we all with laughter.

Before Christmas, occurred my first and last attack of illness in the Crimea. It was not of much consequence, nor should I mention it but to show the kindness of my soldier friends. I think it arose from the sudden commencement of winter, for which I was but poorly provided.

However, I soon received much sympathy and many presents of warm clothing etc., but the most delicate piece of attention was shown me by one of the Sappers and Miners, who, hearing the report that I was dead, positively came down to Spring Hill to take my measure for a coffin.

This may seem a questionable compliment, but I really felt flattered and touched with such a mark of thoughtful attention. Very few in the Crimea had the luxury of any better coffin than a blanket shroud and it was very good of the grateful fellow to determine that his old friend, the mistress of Spring Hill, should have an honour conceded to so very few of the illustrious dead at Sebastopol.

So Christmas came and with it pleasant memories of home and home comforts. With it came also news of home — some not of the most pleasant description — and kind wishes from absent friends.

A merry Christmas to you, writes one, *and many of them. Although you will not write to us, we see your name frequently in the newspapers, from which we judge that you are strong and hearty All your old Jamaica friends are delighted to hear of you and say that you are an honour to the Isle of Springs.*

I wonder if the people of other countries are as fond of carrying with them everywhere the home habits as the English. I think not. I think there was something purely and essentially English in the determination of the camp to spend the Christmas day of 1855 after the good old 'home' fashion. It showed itself weeks before the eventful day. In the dinner parties which were got up, in the orders sent to England, in the supplies which came out, and in the many applications made to the hostess of the British Hotel for plum puddings and mince pies. The demand for them and the material necessary to manufacture them was marvellous. I can fancy that if returns could be got at of the flour, plums, currants and eggs consumed on Christmas Day in the out of the way Crimean peninsula, they would astonish us. One determination appeared to have taken possession of every mind — to spend the festive day with the mirth and jollity which the changed prospect of affairs warranted and the recollection of a year ago, when death and misery were the camp's chief guests, only served to heighten this resolve.

For three weeks previous to Christmas Day, my time was fully occupied in making preparations for it. Pages of my books are filled with orders for plum puddings and mince pies, besides which I sold an immense quantity of raw material to those who were too far off to send down for the manufactured article on the day. To such purchasers I gave a plain recipe for their guidance. Will the reader take any interest in my Crimean Christmas pudding? It was plain, but decidedly good. However, you shall judge for yourself:

1 pound of flour
3/4 of a pound of raisins,
3/4 of a pound of fat pork, chopped fine
2 tablespoonfuls of sugar
a little cinnamon or chopped lemon
1/2 pint of milk or water
Mix these well together and boil 4 hours.

From an early hour in the morning until long after the night had set in, were I and my cooks busy endeavouring to supply the great demand for Christmas fare. We had considerable difficulty in keeping our engagements, but by substituting mince pies for plum puddings, in a few cases, we succeeded. The scene in the crowded store and even in the little overheated kitchen with the officers' servants who came in for their masters' dinners, cannot well be described.

Some were impatient themselves, others dreaded their masters' impatience as the appointed dinner hour passed by — all combined by entreaties, threats, cajolery and fun to drive me distracted. Angry cries for the major's plum pudding, which was to have been ready an hour ago, alternated with an entreaty that I should cook the captain's mince pies to a turn.

"Sure, he likes them well done, ma'am. Bake 'em as brown as your own pretty face, darlin'."

I did not get my dinner until eight o'clock, when I dined in peace off a fine wild turkey, shot for me on the marshes by the Tchernaya. It weighed twenty-two pounds and, although somewhat coarse in colour, had a capital flavour.

Upon New Year's Day I had another large cooking of plum puddings and mince pies, this time upon my own account. I took them to the hospital of the Land Transport Corps, to remind the patients of the home comforts they longed so much for. It was a sad sight to see the once fine fellows, in their blue gowns, lying quiet and still and reduced to such a level of weakness and helplessness. They all seemed glad for the little home tokens I took them.

There was one patient who had been a most industrious and honest fellow and who did not go into the hospital until long and wearing illness compelled him. I was particularly anxious to look after him, but I found him very weak and ill. I stayed with him until evening and before I left him, kind fancy had brought to his bedside his wife and children from his village home in England and I could hear him talking to them in a low and joyful tone. Poor, poor fellow! The New Year so full of hope and happiness had dawned upon him, but he did not live to see the wild flowers spring up peacefully through the wartrodden mud of Sebastopol!

CHAPTER 19

Before the New Year was far advanced we all began to think of going home, making sure that peace would soon be concluded. And never did more welcome message come anywhere than that which brought us intelligence of the armistice and the firing, which had grown more and more slack lately, ceased altogether. Of course, the army did not desire peace because they had any distaste for fighting, far from it. I believe the only more welcome intelligence would have been news of a campaign in the field, but they were most heartily weary of sieges and the prospect of another year before the gloomy north of Sebastopol dampened the ardour of the most sanguine.

Before the armistice was signed, the Russians and their old foes made advances of friendship and the banks of the Tchernaya used to be thronged with soldiers and many strange acquaintances were thus began. I was one of the first to ride down to the Tchernaya and very much delighted seemed the Russians to see an English woman. I wonder if they thought they all had my complexion. I soon entered heartily with the Russians into the then current amusement — that of exchanging coins. I stole a march upon my companions by making the sign of the cross upon my bosom, upon which a Russian threw me, in exchange for some few pence, a little metal figure of some ugly saint. There was a great traffic going on in such things and a wag of an officer, who could talk Russian imperfectly, set himself to work to persuade an innocent Russian that I was his wife and, having succeeded in doing so, promptly offered to dispose of me in exchange for the medal hanging at the Russian's breast.

The last firing of any consequence was the salutes with which the good tidings of peace were received by army and navy. After this soon began the homegoing with happy faces and light hearts and some kind thoughts and warm tears for the comrades left behind.

I was very glad to hear of peace also, although it must have been apparent to everyone that it would cause our financial ruin. We had lately made extensive additions to our store and outhouses — our shelves were filled with articles laid in at a great cost and which were now unsaleable, and which it would be equally impossible to carry home. Everything, from our stud of horses and mules down to our latest consignments from home, must be sold for any price. As it happened, for many things worth a year ago their weight in gold, no purchaser could now be found. However, more of this hereafter.

Before leaving the Crimea, I made various excursions into the interior, visiting Simpheropol and Baktchiserai. I travelled to Simpheropol with a pretty large party and had a very amusing journey. My companions were young and full of fun and tried hard to persuade the Prussians that I was Queen Victoria, by paying me the most absurd reverence. When this failed they fell back a little and declared that I was the Queen's first cousin. Anyhow, they attracted crowds about me and I became quite a lioness in the streets of Simpheropol, until the arrival of some Highlanders in their uniform cut me out.

My excursion to Baktchiserai was still more amusing and pleasant. I found it necessary to go to beat up a Russian merchant who, after the declaration of peace, had purchased stores from us and was refusing to pay for them. Some young officers made up a party for the purpose. We hired an araba, filled it with straw and some boxes to sit upon and set out very early, with two old umbrellas to shield us from the midday sun and the night dews. We had with us a hamper carefully packed before parting, with a cold duck, some cold meat, a tart etc. We rolled on until midday, when, thoroughly exhausted, we left our clumsy vehicle and carried our hamper beneath the shade of a beautiful cherry tree and determined to lunch. Upon opening it the first thing that met our eyes was a fine rat, who made a speedy escape. Somewhat gravely, we proceeded to unpack its contents, without caring to express our fears to one another and quite soon enough we found them realized. How or where the rat had gained access to our hamper it was impossible to say, but he had made no bad use of his time and both wings of the cold duck had flown, while the tart was considerably mangled. Sad discovery this for people who, although hungry, were still squeamish. We made out as well as we could with the cold beef and gave the rest to our Tartar driver, who had apparently no disinclination to eating after the rat, and would very likely have despised us heartily for such weakness. After dinner we went on more briskly and succeeded in reaching Baktchiserai.

My journey was perfectly unavailing. I could not find my debtor at home and if I had I was told it would take three weeks before the Russian law would assist me to recover my claim. Determined, however, to have some compensation, I carried off a raven, which had been croaking angrily at my intrusion. Before we had been long on our homeward journey, however, Lieut. C. sat upon it, of course accidentally, and we threw it to its relatives — the crows.

As the spring advanced, the troops began to move away at a brisk pace. As they passed the Iron House upon the Col — old for the Crimea — where so much of life's action had been compressed into so short a space of time, they would stop and give us a parting cheer, while very often the band struck up some familiar tune of that home they were so gladly seeking. Very often the kind-hearted officers would find time to run into the British Hotel to bid us goodbye and give us a farewell shake of the hand, for you see war, like death, is a great leveller and mutual suffering and endurance had made us all friends.

My dear Mrs. Seacole and my dear Mr. Day, wrote one on a scrap of paper left on the counter, *I have called here four times this day, to wish you goodbye. I am so sorry I was not fortunate enough to see you. I shall still hope to see you tomorrow morning. We march at seven a.m.*

And yet all this going home seemed strange and somewhat sad. Sometimes I felt that I could not sympathise with the glad faces and happy hearts of those who were looking forward to the delights of home and the joy of seeing once more the old familiar faces remembered so fondly in the fearful trenches and the hard-fought battlefields. Now and then we would see a lounger with a blank face, taking no interest in the bustle of departure and with him I acknowledged to have more fellow feeling than with the others, for he, as well as I, clearly had no home to go to. He was a soldier by choice and necessity, as well as by profession. He had no home, no loved friends, the peace would bring no particular pleasure to him, whereas war and action were necessary to his existence, gave him excitement, occupation, the chance of promotion.

Now and then, but seldom however, you came across such a disappointed one. Was it not so with me? Had I not been happy through the months of toil and danger, never knowing what fear or depression was, finding every moment of the day mortgaged hours in advance and earning sound sleep and contentment by sheer hard work? What better or happier lot could possibly befall me? And, alas, how likely was it that, my present occupation gone, I might long in vain for another so stirring and so useful. Besides which, it was pretty sure that I should go to England poorer than I left it, an although I was not ashamed of poverty, beginning life again in the autumn — I mean late in the summer of life — is hard uphill work.

Peace concluded, the little jealousies which may have sprung up between the French and their allies seemed forgotten and everyone was anxious, ere the parting came, to make the most of the time yet left in improving old friendships and founding new. Among others, the 47th encamped near the Woronzoff Road, gave a grand parting entertainment to a large company of their French neighbours, at which many officers of high rank were present. I was applied to by the committee of management to superintend the affair and, for the last time in the Crimea, the health of Madame Seacole was proposed and duly honoured. I had grown so accustomed to the honour that I had no difficulty in returning thanks in a speech which Colonel B. interpreted amid roars of laughter to the French guests.

As the various regiments moved off, I received many acknowledgments from those who thought they owed me gratitude. Little presents, warm farewell words, kind letters full of grateful acknowledgments for services so small that I had forgotten them long, long ago — how easy it is to reach warm hearts! — little thoughtful acts of kindness, even from the humblest. And these touched me the most. I value the letters received from the men far more than the testimonials of their officers.

But I had other friends in the Crimea — friends who could never thank me. Some of them lay in their last sleep, beneath indistinguishable mounds of earth, some in the half-filled trenches, a few beneath the blue waters of the Euxine. I might in vain attempt to gather the wild flowers which sprung up above many of their graves, but I knew where some lay and could visit their last homes on earth. And to all the cemeteries where friends rested so calmly, sleeping well after a life's work nobly done, I went many times, lingering long over many a mound that bore the names of those whom I had been familiar with in life, thinking of what they had been and what I had known of them. Over some I planted shrubs and flowers, little lilac trees, obtained with no small trouble and flowering evergreens, which looked quite gay and pretty ere I left and may in time become great trees and witness strange scenes, or be cut down as fuel for another besieging army — who can tell? And from many graves I picked up pebbles and plucked simple wildflowers, or tufts of grass, as memorials for relatives at home.

How pretty the cemeteries used to look beneath the blue peaceful sky, neatly enclosed with stone walls and full of the gravestones reared by friends over friends. I met many here, thoughtfully taking their last look of the resting places of those they knew and loved. I saw many a proud head bowed down above them. I knew that many a proud heart laid aside its pride here and stood in the presence of death, humble and childlike. And by the clasped hand and moistened eye, I knew that from many a heart sped upward a grateful prayer to the Providence which had thought fit in his judgment to take some and in his mercy to spare the rest.

Some three weeks before the Crimea was finally evacuated, we moved from our old quarters to Balaclava, where we had obtained permission to fit up a store for the short time which would elapse before the last red coat left Russian soil. The poor old British Hotel! We could do nothing with it. The iron house was pulled down and packed up for conveyance home, but the Russians got all of the outhouses and sheds which was not used as fuel. All the kitchen fittings and stoves that had cost us so much, fell also into their hands. I only wish some cook worthy to possess them has them now. We could sell nothing. Our horses were almost given away, our large stores of provisions were at anyone's service. It makes my heart sick to talk of the really alarming sacrifices we made. The Russians crowded down ostensibly to purchase, in reality to plunder. Prime cheeses, which had cost us tenpence a pound, were sold to them for less than a penny a pound. Wine for which we had paid forty-eight shillings a dozen, they bid four shillings. I could not stand this and, in a fit of desperation, I snatched up a hammer and broke up case after case, while the bystanders held out their hands and caught the ruby stream. It may have been wrong, but I was too excited to think. There was no more of my own people to give it to and I would rather not present it to our old foes.

We were among the last to leave the Crimea. Before going I borrowed a horse, easy enough now, and rode up the old well-known road — how unfamiliar in its loneliness and quiet — to Cathcart's Hill. I wished once more to impress the scene upon my mind. It was a beautifully clear evening and we could see miles away across the darkening sea. I spent some time there with my companions, pointing out to each other the sites of scenes we all remembered so well. There were the trenches, already becoming indistinguishable, out of which, on the 8th of September, we had seen the storming parties tumble in confused and scattered bodies, before they ran up the broken height of the Redan. There the Malakhoff, into which we had also seen the luckier French pour in one unbroken seam. Below lay the crumbling city and the quiet harbour, with scarce a ripple on its surface, while around stretched away the deserted huts for miles. It was with something like regret that we said to one another that the play was fairly over, that peace had brought the curtain down and that we, humble actors in some of its most stirring scenes, must seek engagement elsewhere.

I lingered behind and, stooping down, once more gathered little tufts of grass and some simple blossoms from above the graves of some who in life had been very kind to me. I left behind, in exchange, a few tears which were sincere.

A few days later, I stood on board a crowded steamer, taking my last look of the shores of the Crimea.

CONCLUSION.

I did not return to England by the most direct route, but took the opportunity of seeing other lands. When I finally arrived we set to work at Aldershot to retrieve our fallen fortunes and stem off the ruin originated in the Crimea, but all in vain. Eventually defeated by fortune, but not I think disgraced, we were obliged to capitulate on very honourable conditions. In plain truth, the old Crimean firm of Seacole and Day was dissolved and its partners had to recommence the world anew. So ended our campaign.

One of us started the other day for the Antipodes, while the other is ready to take any journey to any place where a stout heart and two experienced hands may be of use.

Perhaps it would be right if I were to express more shame and annoyance than I really feel at the pecuniarily disastrous issue of my Crimean adventures, but I cannot. When I would try and feel ashamed of being poor and helpless, I only experience a glow of pride at the more pleasing events of my career. I cannot help remembering also the many who profess themselves indebted to me.

Let me, in as few words as possible, state the results of my Crimean campaign. To be sure, I returned from it shaken in health. I came home wounded, as many others did. Few constitutions, indeed, were the better for those winters before Sebastopol and I was too hard worked not to feel their effects, for a little labour fatigues me now — I cannot watch by sickbeds as I could — a week's want of rest quite knocks me up now. Then I returned bankrupt in fortune. Whereas others in my position may have come back to England rich and prosperous, I found myself poor — beggared. So few words can tell what I have lost.

What have I gained? I should need a volume to begin, so much is it and so cheaply purchased by suffering ten times worse than what I have experienced. Wherever I go I am sure to meet some smiling face in the crowded London streets, forgotten by me, perhaps, but who soon reminds me of our life in Sebastopol. In omnibuses, in river steamboats, in places of public amusement spring up old familiar faces to remind me of the months spent on Spring Hill. The sentries at Whitehall relax from the discharge of their important duty of guarding nothing, to give me a smile of recognition. The very newspaper offices look friendly as I pass them by; busy Printinghouse Yard puts on a cheering smile and the *Punch* office in Fleet Street sometimes laughs outright. Now, would all this have happened if I had returned to England a rich woman? Surely not.

A few words more before I bring these egotistical remarks to a close. It is naturally with feelings of pride and pleasure that I allude to the committee recently organized to aid me, and if I indulge in the vanity of placing their names before my readers, it is simply because every one of the following noblemen and gentlemen knew me in the Crimea and by consenting to assist me now record publicly their opinion of my services there. And yet I may reasonably on other grounds be proud of the fact, that it has been stated publicly that my present embarrassments originated in my charities and incessant labours among the army.

END